PRAISE FOR *SOAR*

"Copying what the competition is doing doesn't work in any industry, especially in air travel which most consumers see as a commodity. Shashank takes a deep dive into the fascinating stories of how successful airlines have created their own path."

— DAVID MEERMAN SCOTT
bestselling author of The New Rules of Marketing and PR,
now in 25 languages from Arabic to Vietnamese.

"Shashank's book SOAR reads very well, and gives the feeling of a longtime friend dispensing wisdom, sharing advice, and motivating you to do your best. It's not a dreary lecture, but rather SOAR is entertaining storytelling that pushes us to fly higher and stronger with our employees, brands, and customers."

— JAY SORENSEN
President, IdeaWorksCompany

"This is the first book to have uncovered and consolidated the best practices in airline marketing. A must-read for anyone looking to build a career in commercial aviation"

— DR. MARIO HARDY
CEO, PATA

"*SOAR* gives you the blueprint for designing long lasting brands. Shashank rocks: read It now, before the airline that competes with you does."

"Shashank Nigam's vision is fully expressed by his analysis of these powerful connections between these airline brands, their customers and their employees. He is the leading steward pushing the boundaries of airline marketing, a pioneer to do so."

"You feel it in the near-perfection customer service of Singapore Girls, when Tony Fernandes replies to your tweet or when you hear Herb Kelleher laugh. Nigam reveals how the best airlines in the world create lasting bonds."

"I've learnt a great deal from Shashank, and you will too. His book uncovers the secrets of the best airline brands in the world, which will help your airline stay ahead of competition, for a long time to come."

— NICOLA LANGE
Director - Premium Services, Lufthansa

"*SOAR* brings home the importance of creativity and empowerment in developing a successful airline brand. It's a great reminder that allowing people to think big can create a strong connection with your customers."

— MARY ELLEN JONES
VP Americas Sales, Pratt & Whitney,
President of The Wings Club

"A classical airline is a commodity business that requires good execution, which many do. The airlines covered in *SOAR* get it that this business is consumer focused, brand-oriented now – it is they who will dominate the 21st century travel."

— MARK LAPIDUS
CEO, Amedeo

"Shashank Nigam gets it: to build a lasting brand, you can't be following the usual rules of marketing. Like the airlines covered in the book, you need to think beyond the ordinary."

— **PATRICK MURPHY**
former Chairman, Ryanair

"The airline industry is very unique. Yet, few have been able to distill lessons from the best airline brands for the rest of us, like Shashank does."

— **HENRI COURPRON**
Former CEO, ILFC and Airbus North America

"One of those rare books that's full of inspiring stories and actionable strategies, which can help you excel in your job as a marketer"

— **DR. BERND SCHMITT**
Author, Director - Center on Global Brand Leadership,
Columbia Business School

"*SOAR* gives you a powerful blueprint for building an airline brand. Its a must read for anyone working with an airline."

— **ALLEN ADAMSON**
former Chairman, North America, Landor

"When an authority on aviation marketing like Shashank authors a book on the topic, you must read it."

"Shashank adds 21st century insight into what can make a difference in what is one of the most competitive and fastest moving sectors there is."

"*SOAR* is a brilliant investigation of how airline brands that succeed do so. Great inspiration if you're in an industry that is just as competitive."

"Airline brands depend on fantastic customer experience, delivered by engaged, empathetic and customer-focused employees. *SOAR* tells the story of seven airlines that have really learned how to do this, and as such, is essential reading for airline executives and those that wish to become airline executives."

SOAR

SOAR

HOW THE WORLD'S BEST AIRLINE BRANDS DELIGHT CUSTOMERS AND INSPIRE EMPLOYEES

SHASHANK NIGAM
WITH MATTHEW SHARPE

IDEAPRESS
PUBLISHING

IDEAPRESS PUBLISHING
www.ideapresspublishing.com

Cover Design by Faceout

Layout Design by Jessica Angerstein

ISBN: 978-1-940858-14-2 (Print)
ISBN: 978-1-940858-14-2 (eBook)

PROUDLY PRINTED IN THE UNITED STATES OF AMERICA By Selby
Marketing Associates

SPECIAL SALES
IdeaPress Books are available at a special discount for bulk purchases
for sales promotions and premiums, or for use in corporate training
programs. Special editions, including personalized covers, custom
forewords, corporate imprints and bonus content are also available.
For more details, email info@ideapresspublishing.com.

*No animals were harmed in the writing, printing or distribution of this book.
The trees, unfortunately, were not so lucky.*

To Don for believing in me when SimpliFlying
was just a figment of my imagination.
To Laird Robin for helping me push the boundaries.
To Daddy for always asking the tough questions.

CONTENTS

—·—

AUTHOR'S NOTE:
CAN A POWERFUL BRAND REALLY MAKE AN AIRLINE MORE PROFITABLE?

At the pre-launch party SOAR in London in September 2016, about one hundred aviation industry executives and journalists received special preview copies of this book. Among the audience was a Senior Lecturer and Course Director of Aviation Management at Coventry University in the UK named Dr. James Pearson. While I had not met him before, I was keen to receive some critical feedback from a professor. And I did. About a month after receiving the book he posted on LinkedIn, "I'm always wary of such books as I like numbers. Who cares if an airline has a brilliant brand with exceptional buy-in if it makes a loss or underperforms financially?"

My original intent when shortlisting airlines to be featured in this book, was to select a global spread of airlines that have each built enduring brands over a long period – from Southwest and Finnair to Air New Zealand and Kulula. I also ensured that of the airlines in this book, half were low-cost carriers and half were legacy airlines. What I had not done was specifically evaluate the financial performance of the shortlisted airlines before approaching them to be featured in the book. This is, after all, a book about building a great brand. So reading Dr. Pearson's comment did pique my curiosity. If creating a powerful brand for the airlines I featured was truly valuable, then shouldn't those airlines deliver better financial results?

Being a quantitative person, Dr. Pearson went on to answer his own question – through an in-depth analysis of the financial performance of all of the airlines featured in this book. His findings were revealing, but not surprising.

Analyzing the financial results of airlines featured in SOAR between 2006 and 2015, Dr. Pearson found that their average operating margin was 5.9%. Compared to the global average of 3.4% in that period, the airlines in this book had an operating margin that was 73.5% higher. It is important to note that this was a period that included record fuel prices and a major global financial crisis. In the last three years, this differential goes up to 87%. His analysis was reassuring, not only for me – but also as a validation for the ideas in this book.

As Dr. Pearson's analysis showed, airlines that give importance to building their brand equity do not necessarily trade off financial performance. In fact, one seems clearly related to the other. The good news is, in the early months of talking about the book before release, Dr. Pearson is hardly the only expert to hold his or her critical lens up to the ideas in this book.

Early momentum for the book

Of those who received the initial copies of the book at my launch event in London, quite a few have written personally to me or shared on social media channels their own reviews of the ideas in the book. One of the executives I interviewed in SOAR, for example, mentioned how he is going to take steps to change internal culture within his team to one that's similar to Air New Zealand's. Another wrote to me saying that his daughter finally understands what her dad does for a living. The positive feedback is heartening.

Early reviews from the media have also been kind. Flight's Airline Business called SOAR a "Simpli must read book" in their review. APEX wrote that this book, "aims to help its readers shake off old ways of thinking, adopt new attitudes and seize opportunities in brand marketing." Formia, a maker of in-flight amenity kits, even invited me to meet with their top apparel executives on how to creatively partner with airlines, having been inspired to do so after reading SOAR. All of the positive momentum and early validation from the industry is humbling and excited for me as an author.

Perhaps more importantly, it signals that the ideas in this book are not only relevant for explaining the importance of building a top notch airline brand – but also the lessons that executives in any industry can learn from some of the aviation industry's best examples.

I hope you enjoy the book and I look forward to connecting further with you!

Shashank Nigam
shashank@simpliflying.com
Toronto, Canada
November 2016

INTRODUCTION

SOAR : sôr/ verb
1. Fly or rise high in the air.
2. Maintain height in the air without flapping wings or using engine power.

In the seven years since I left my job in Boston to start SimpliFlying, I have flown just over a million miles on 91 airlines. A number of these flights have been on the three major U.S. carriers—American Airlines, United Airlines, and Delta Air Lines. What's amazing is that while I remember being on these airlines, I don't quite recall when I was on which. It's not that I have a failing memory—I do remember most of my flights and destinations quite well—but these three airlines just seemed very similar to one another every time I have flown with them. It is as if all three of the largest U.S. airlines are trying very hard to be unremarkable.

All three have blue and grey interiors. All three have tight seats in economy class—they all call it coach—served by seemingly disinterested flight attendants. When one skews the frequent flier program toward only the top-tier elite, the other two do as well, and the majority of fliers suffer.

Things don't stand out if you're flying business class either. Lounges are often just overcrowded rooms with a selection of snacks so unappetizing that they are available in abundance. When one of the three airlines announces flat beds on cross-continental flights in response to the likes of JetBlue, the other two follow suit soon after. However, scant attention is paid to improving the standard of service. "The big three airlines have dissolved into one big homogeneous blob," said industry analyst Henry Harteveldt, founder of Atmosphere Research Group, a travel-industry survey and consulting firm, in a recent article in the *Wall Street Journal*. In the airline business, it is easy to follow one another into mediocrity.

On the other hand, there is one domestic flight I distinctly remember. I was on a late-night flight from Chicago to Austin, Texas, to attend a conference. We were landing just before midnight. As the flight attendants took their seats for landing, one of them came on the microphone, and to my surprise, sang a spontaneous lullaby for us as we landed. She explained she was used to singing it every night to her kids, anyway. It was a refreshing end to the day for most of the passengers, who clapped to thank the flight attendant once we landed. That was my first flight with Southwest, back in 2010 and it left an indelible impression.

Most airlines seem to be trying to provide us with an uneventful flight that gets us from point A to B. Yet Southwest stood out, just by being itself, and not trying too hard. For example, most airlines today charge you to check a bag, and charge you even more to check two, following the lead of the likes of United. Southwest has not charged for a bag since it started operations and it has stuck to its guns while the rest of the industry took a big step backward in a blind pursuit of ancillary revenues. It was a little like *Charlie and the Chocolate Factory*, where Charlie ultimately wins because the rest have dug their own graves. Amazingly, it is not just the major U.S. airline brands that are placing a greater burden on passengers, but airlines large and small around the world. That's why the Southwests of the world stand out.

While most of my flights are a blur, some have been unforgettable.

I'll never forget when the flight attendant on my AirAsia flight from Singapore to Kuala Lumpur was walking down the aisle to do her in-flight safety checks, noticed that I was reading a book, and took the time to turn on my reading light. Or when the Singapore Girl addressed me by name, despite my being the last to board the flight. Or the time when Finnair displayed a custom-designed Northern Lights projection aboard its Airbus A350 upon take off from New York. What do these airlines have in common? How do they become remarkable? Each one has developed a unique formula that enables its brand to leave a lasting, positive impression on its customers—and to attract new customers as well. During my 2,000 hours in the air—and many more on the ground—I've studied the branding successes and failures of the 91 airlines I've flown, and I've developed a model that enables me to analyze the six major elements that will make or break any airline brand. I call it the 6X Airline Brand Model.

The 6X Airline Brand Model

My consulting firm, SimpliFlying, began its journey when I realized that marketing an airline is distinctly different from marketing any other product or service. For example, our brand engagement with a can of Coke lasts about 10 minutes. With a cup of Starbucks coffee, perhaps an hour. But with an airline, our brand engagement can last anywhere from 2 to 24 hours, depending on how long the flight is. Add in the online booking process and other pre-travel phases, and we realize that aviation brands have many times the number of touchpoints of brands in other sectors. Moreover, if there is a snowstorm and we are in Starbucks, the coffee tastes just as good. But if we are at an airport and our flight is canceled due to the storm, we are mad at the airline. At that moment, the airline brand cannot brush off the responsibility and say that they are not the cause of the inconvenience. While this may be technically true, an airline that can rise to the occasion will send a strong signal to its customers.

Despite these unique features of airline brand engagement, most airline marketers tend to apply the same generic marketing principles as marketers of other consumer products. Aviation marketing ought to be as distinct from other kinds of marketing as airlines are from other brands. How many times have you seen a beautiful advertisement with a passenger lounging on a flat bed, being served gourmet food? This is far from the reality for a large majority of passengers, who end up at the back of the cabin, packed like sardines and trying to get work done on a laptop, their arms crunched in like a T-rex's. There is seldom a svelte flight attendant putting a duvet over them. Right there, the brand promise fails. Like the major U.S. carriers mentioned earlier, airlines almost always over-promise and under-deliver.

The airline industry is truly like no other. It is cyclical in nature, incurs high fixed costs, faces uncertainties due to heavy dependency on fluctuating factors like weather and oil prices, and has a length of engagement with the customer that is rare in other industries. Hence, a distinctive approach is needed for airline branding that takes into account all these factors unique to the industry.

An ideal branding model for the airlines would account for both the realities of business and the unique nature of the industry. The 6X model helps guide an airline's branding approach by focusing on six key levers:

1. **Brand eXpectation:** how accurately and successfully an airline lets customers know what it has to offer.
2. **Brand eXperience:** what it feels like to interact with the airline during travel, across all touchpoints, at the airport and in-flight.
3. **Brand eXpression:** how well the airline communicates with customers and staff

4. **Brand eXternalities:** anything that affects customers that is not in the control of the airline (weather, oil prices, regulations, etc.).
5. **Brand eXecution:** how an airline delivers on its promises.
6. **Brand X-Factor:** the special sauce possessed exclusively by the airline in question that is hard to duplicate for competition.

In the past seven years, as SimpliFlying has worked with more than 75 airlines and airports around the world, time and again we have seen that airlines that successfully apply these principles create remarkable brands.

The first three levers of the 6X model—eXpectation, eXperience, and eXpression—focus on engagement, internal and external, which is very much in the airline's control. This is the process from brand awareness, to preference and purchase, to the post-purchase brand interactions. The second three levers—eXternalities, eXecution, X-factor—deal with aspects unique to the airlines, which often have a deep impact on the brand. The 6X model specifically avoids a purely quantitative derivation of an airline's brand value, since the brand is an intangible asset and qualitative factors play a major role in building this asset.

If an airline delivers what it promises, interacts with its customers consistently and responsibly over time, and continues to innovate, people will continue to vote for it with their wallets, their respect, and their affection. Today more than ever, as global competition becomes increasingly fierce among commercial carriers, a model like 6X is critical to guide airline executives and help them decide how to build a distinctive and sustainable brand advantage. After all, the last thing they would want is to follow the leader of the pack and do more of the same.

How This Book Works

Every airline featured in *SOAR* is remarkable in one way or another. Each chapter focuses only on one airline and dives deep into how the airline stands out from the crowd. Some are remarkable because of the product offering they have created, like Singapore Airlines or Air New Zealand. Others are remarkable because of a culture that values and empowers employees, like Southwest or AirAsia. Yet others soar above the rest simply by doing things that are unexpected, like Turkish Airlines having a chef serve the meals in business class, or kulula having jokes on its safety cards. At the end of each chapter, I have distilled the key 6X factors the airline excels in. It is important to note that no airline in the book tries to excel on all 6X factors, but instead focuses on achieving standout success in a few of them. That keeps them out of reach of competition, and keeps the passengers coming back.

It is also important to note what *SOAR* is not. It is not a book that provides an exhaustive analysis of each airline's operations or business plans. It is not meant to be an authoritative tome on any one airline. Rather, it is the culmination of detailed conversations with both top executives and customer-facing staff at each of the airlines. As such, *SOAR* focuses on the best practices in marketing from each airline, having learned about them from the people who led them and executed them.

When choosing the airlines to be featured in *SOAR*, we worked hard to ensure a wide global spread of the case studies. Whether you are a student of marketing at a university or a seasoned airline manager eyeing that executive position, I am sure you will be stimulated and inspired by these stories of creativity at airlines around the world. You can choose to read this book cover to cover, or just dive into any chapter at random. At the end of the book, a chapter summarizes the 6X model, which you can re-visit any time. And of course, if you are looking to enhance customer engagement at your airline, please do not hesitate to get in touch with me via our website, simpliflying.com, or email me directly. More resources from the book like, interview transcripts and videos, can be found on www.simplisoar.com. One of the greatest rewards of working on *SOAR* in the last 12 months has been traveling to different airline headquarters, hearing some very interesting stories and meeting people so passionate about the industry. After almost a hundred interviews, I was heartened to see the 6X model being validated time and again. Airline brands featured in this book truly *soar*—they effortlessly glide above the competition, while the rest flap their wings tirelessly to gain altitude below. I hope you enjoy the read.

— Shashank Nigam
   simplisoar@simpliflying.com

1: SOUTHWEST: A LUV STORY

Introduction

In 1983, about a decade after Southwest Airlines started flying, a children's book called *Gumwrappers and Goggles,* written and illustrated by Winifred Barnum, was published. To most readers, the book was largely indistinguishable from the multitude of children's books published each year. But the premise of its story had an uncanny resemblance to a famous court case that anyone following Southwest Airlines would have identified.

In the story, TJ Luv, a small jet, is taken to court by two larger jets to keep him from their hangar and stop him from flying. In 1967, soon after Herb Kelleher and Rollin King incorporated the airline in Texas, three other airlines—Braniff, Trans-Texas, and Continental Airlines—started legal action against Southwest (then called Air Southwest Co.) to prevent it from flying. In the book, TJ Luv's right to fly is upheld after impassioned arguments from a character called The Lawyer. In 1970, Air Southwest prevailed over its antagonists as the courts upheld its right to fly.

While no company names were mentioned in the book (which continues to be in print), TJ Luv's colors were those of Southwest Airlines, and the two other jets were in Braniff and Continental colors. The Lawyer, quite obviously, resembled Herb Kelleher.

Having overcome legal struggles, Air Southwest Co. changed its name to Southwest Airlines Co. in 1971, and established its headquarters in Dallas, Texas. Southwest Airlines began scheduled flights on June 18, 1971, from Dallas' Love Field to Houston, and Dallas to San Antonio, with their fleet of three 737-200s.

One of the greatest airline stories of the modern era was finally underway.

Say it with LUV

The children's book, which turns out to have been commissioned by the airline, is only one of the myriad ways in which Southwest Airlines has affected and shaped its public perception and, in the process, stood out from its competitors. That process, of course, started right at the beginning when Lamar Muse, the airline's first president, ordained that hostesses (all female at the beginning) would be dressed in tangerine hot pants and go-go boots. As Southwest Airlines claims on its website, "With the prettiest Flight Attendants serving 'Love Bites' on our planes, and determined Employees issuing tickets from our 'Love Machines,' we changed the face of the airline industry throughout the 1970s."

The hot pants and go-go boots eventually gave way to less gimmicky, more respectful attire for its female flight attendants. In 1982, Southwest finally decreed that customer-facing agents could be both male and female. The airline, initially a close copy of Pacific Southwest Airlines, developed its own distinct culture and practices, including a unique boarding process. Recently, Southwest has embraced social media wholeheartedly, not only in order to reach out to its many advocates—and to offer a glimpse into the brand—but also to serve its customers better.

Most importantly, the word "Love"—or, in Southwest's orthography, "LUV"—has been important to Southwest's brand from the beginning. TJ Luv is but one small repitition of the LUV theme. The airline claims that "Southwest has been in LUV with our Customers from the very beginning. Therefore, it's fitting that we began service to San Antonio and Houston from Love Field in Dallas on June 18, 1971. As our Company and Customers grew, our LUV grew too! Then in 1977, our stock was listed on the New York Stock Exchange under the ticker symbol 'LUV.' Over the ensuing years, our LUV has spread from coast to coast and border to border thanks to our hardworking Employees and their LUV for Customer Service."

In 2016, Southwest Airlines is at a delicate stage. As the largest domestic carrier in the US, it is in a unique position. It flies to about a 100 destinations, employs over 50,000 people, and has a massive fleet of more than 700 planes all Boeing 737s. It is also the second-largest carrier in the world, transporting almost 144 million passengers in 2015. While other airlines have suffered bankruptcies and layoffs, Southwest has remained profitable for 43 consecutive years.

LUV has brought Southwest Airlines this far. But now that the airline is poised for international growth and further expansion, can LUV thrive globally?

The Brand with a Heart

The Southwest story has become famous in the airline industry and beyond. Yet it grows better with each passing year, as Southwest Airlines itself grows. It starts like this: More than 49 years ago, Rollin King and Herb Kelleher decided to start a different kind of airline. They began with one simple notion: if you get your passengers to their destinations when they want to get there, on time, at the lowest possible fares, and make darn sure they have a good time doing it, people will fly your airline.

Herb was later joined by Colleen Barrett, who had been his executive assistant at the law firm he ran before starting Southwest. Working closely with her mentor and former boss, Colleen pioneered Southwest's unusual and now legendary approach to customer service, which aims to treat the company's employees like family, to make the workplace fun, and then to carry that upbeat attitude to consumers.

Everything that Southwest has done since its inception has aimed to prove that it's possible to succeed through a dedication to the highest quality of customer service delivered with a "sense of warmth, friendliness, individual pride, and company spirit."

Employees Embody the Brand

Though she stepped down from active duty in 2008, speak to employees now and you get a sense that Colleen's spirit is still at the center of the airline's ethos. "Everyone cares, everyone is cared for" is a motto that resonates with the airline's staff. Almost everyone we spoke to had a reverential attitude toward their former boss.

Mike Hafner, Vice President of Cabin Services, says that little has changed in the last 35 years. Mike has been in the airline business since age 15, when he began working out of the back of his mother's station wagon as a baggage delivery agent for several airlines. He began working at Southwest in 1981, when he was just 23 years old. His first job was ramp agent, cleaning the planes when they stayed overnight in Austin, Texas. In 1982, after it was decreed that flight crew and ticket agents could be both male and female, Mike became the second male ticket agent in Southwest history. For 26 years, he held multiple positions in ground operations before becoming the Vice President of Inflight Services in 2007. In 2009, wanting to enhance customer experience, Mike led the effort to combine Inflight and Provisioning into the single Cabin Services department, adding another 14,000 people to his responsibilities almost overnight. Since 2015, he has been Vice President of Customer Services. He describes Southwest employees' trajectory at the airline not as a ladder, but as a lattice, since the airline encourages employees not simply to move up the ranks within a single department, but to move their talents from one department to another, resulting in people with a greater-than-usual breadth of knowledge of the industry.

Southwest is still an organization that believes in creating strong leaders who care about their teams. In fact, the reason Southwest has succeeded, according to Mike, is that "both its leaders and its frontline employees have outworked and outcared the competition."

Brand Refresh

One of the people who most exemplify outworking and outcaring is Anne Murry, who led the brand refresh and rollout for Southwest Airlines in 2014. After extensive research and concept evaluations that stressed the need to appear fresh while retaining the spirit of Southwest, Anne and her team put love right at the center of the brand.

Research started in 2013 with both customers and non-customers. The focus was on remaining a colorful brand. Also a consistent brand: before then there had been no brand guide. Everything was completely dependent on trust. Internally there was no brand consistency, with different departments carrying out different executions of internal campaigns. So the custom logo used for a community day effort, for instance, was different from the custom logo for a birthday party.

The previous update to the brand had happened in 2001, and was minor compared with the thoroughgoing 2013 effort. This time everything was re-examined, and every element of the brand that was retained or created anew had to have a good reason to exist. In a logo redesign, the word "Airlines" was dropped entirely. Anne cites Apple and Starbucks as inspirations: Apple removed the word

"Computers" from its logo and Starbucks went so far as to remove the word "Starbucks." The "Southwest" is now followed by a small heart, almost like a punctuation mark, signifying humility. The desire was, ultimately, to position Southwest as a lifestyle brand, with heart at its core.

The Southwest ride has been exhilarating for Anne, with many high points, but the night of the brand rollout, September 8, 2014, was particularly special for her. She still gets emotional when recalling it. After Dallas Love Field had ended its day at around 2:30 a.m., a team moved into place and flipped the images at 4:00 a.m. Anne describes it as a magical night, reminiscent of Christmas, in which gifts were unwrapped one by one. The team was in tears, hugging and kissing each other, savoring the moment they'd awaited for months.

She also remembers sighing with relief after it was all over. So much could have gone wrong, but everything went right. She says, "It's the people I get to work with, it blows my mind, that's why I've stayed in a marketing role for 25 years."

Responses to the new brand from customers were mostly very positive. Respondents singled out the heart in the logo: no other airline has it, and it probably would not feel right as a brand statement about any airline but Southwest.

Even when introducing the world to something so obviously customer-targeted as a new brand identity, Southwest ensured that its core values would still drive the change. This is how Gary Kelly, current CEO of Southwest, introduced the re-branding: "Our collective heartbeat is stronger and healthier than ever, and that's because of the warmth, the compassion, and the smiles of our People. The Heart emblazoned on our aircraft, and within our new look, symbolizes our commitment that we'll remain true to our core values as we set our sights on the future."

People Power

Southwest Airlines has consistently won accolades for being one of the best companies to work at. Not only that, but it is usually the only airline on such lists. A positive culture has been a crucial part of the company's DNA all along. As Herb Kelleher put it, "The business of business is people, people, and people." For Southwest, that was true in the beginning, it is true today, and it will hopefully be true in the coming years. You will hear statements from Herb like this repeated often at Southwest: "Our people make us what and who we are, and our people can deliver what our customers want and need."

To achieve and maintain its people-centered approach, Southwest begins with a set of attributes that percolate through the organization. Enter Southwest's offices and you'll invariably find a poster reminding employees of three desirable traits that encapsulate the Southwest way: "Warrior Spirits, Servant's Hearts, Fun-LUVing Attitudes."

Each of these three traits has helpful sub-traits to ensure the message of the bold headlines is backed up with specifics. According to Julie Weber, VP of People at Southwest (at other organizations she would be known as VP of Human Resources), a Warrior Spirit means "a desire to excel, act with courage, persevere, and innovate." A Servant's Heart entails "the ability to put others first, treat everyone with respect, and proactively serve customers." And a fun-loving attitude includes "passion, joy, and an aversion to taking oneself too seriously."

"Hire for Attitude, Train for Skill"

These are not mere commandments that sit desolately on walls. Employees at Southwest have been nursed and nurtured into living by them. In fact, if they do not already embody them, they are unlikely to be hired. To ensure that they get the sort of people who embody Southwest traits, Southwest uses a behavior-based interviewing process. Potential recruits are asked questions that determine whether their past job performance indicates a dedication to service, creativity, and problem-solving skills.

Says Shari Conaway, who has been at the airline for 22 years in the People department, "At Southwest, we hire for attitude and train for skill." In other words, it does not matter if the new hire's previous profession was not airline-related. If candidates score high marks in the Warrior, Servant, and Fun categories, they are likely to fit the Southwest mold. Shari says it is easier to train someone from another field how an airline works than it is to train someone from aviation how to be a nice person. In fact, the organization likes having a staff with diverse employment backgrounds, since a diversity of ideas will help improve the business.

Southwest spends an unusual amount of time on the recruiting and hiring process, and the numbers show how tough it is to land a job there. In 2015, the airline reviewed more than 351,000 resumes, interviewed close to 130,000 potential candidates, and hired just over 6,300 new employees. It is typical for the airline to interview more than 100 people to fill a single position. A fact often repeated with pride is that statistically it's harder to get into Southwest than it is to get into Harvard.

One of the most unusual ideas that float around with an air of normalcy at Southwest is something that would sound outrageous elsewhere: "At Southwest we are family. Hence nepotism makes sense," said Gary Kelly, the CEO. Many Southwest employees are spouses or children of other Southwest employees. The airline actively encourages family members to apply for vacancies. While there are safeguards, such as not allowing one family member to supervise another, Southwest seeks to harness the potential of kin who are already familiar with and invested in the brand—those who have grown up hearing about it, and know the benefits of being employed there. For example, VP of Cabin Services Mike Hafner's brother works at Southwest, and so does his wife—in fact, he met his wife on the job. Connor Hughey, who works in Customer Relations at Southwest, completed two years with the company in June 2016. Not coincidentally, his mother, Cheryl Hughey, has been with Southwest for 36 years, and is now Managing Director of Culture. Connor says he "grew up with the company" and was already familiar with the Southwest ethos when he joined. Seeing his mom work so dedicatedly with the airline encouraged him to seek a position there.

Building a Sense of Community

In 1999, Mike Hafner was diagnosed with a brain tumor, and underwent an operation the following year. He remembers receiving handwritten notes and cards from people in the organization, many of whom had probably never even met him. While he was in the hospital, his wife was compelled to stay home and tend to her pregnancy. Mike's sister-in-law, who worked at United, came to help. One day while she was attending to Mike at the hospital, she read all the notes. Overwhelmed, she started weeping. At that moment she understood how different Southwest was from United, where she'd always felt like just another number.

Mike says Southwest understands that every employee has a story. The job of leaders is to learn those stories and through them, connect on a human level with their teams.

The sense of community at Southwest was put to a test when in 2014 the company acquired AirTran Airways, another low-cost airline based in Atlanta, Georgia. This was Southwest's first acquisition of another airline. It was an anxious time for many at Southwest, who were concerned about dilution of the culture, quality of incoming staff (remember Southwest's two-percent hiring rate) and pay disparities with AirTran employees who would suddenly start earning more at Southwest compared to their original pay.

The leadership at Southwest took the situation by the horns, and did what they do best—they harnessed the power of people. They initiated community programs to integrate AirTran employees and show them the Southwest Way. For the induction, a Wingmate program was established. Every AirTran employee brought in was paired with a Southwest buddy who would act as a coach-mentor-friend and show the new employee the ropes of the organization. Second, a Read Before Lead program ensured that the same information about the acquisition was shared across all Southwest leaders. The purpose of Read Before Lead was to ensure transparency, so that no corrosive rumors were floated about the acquisition. Third, under the Sponsor a New Hire initiative, Southwest would get its employees to pay five dollars to sponsor the lanyard of a new person for the induction training. In addition, photos of all new hires were displayed on a wall on the walls of the training center, and every new hire received a handwritten note from a current Southwest employee. The Wingmate program was later extended for a year, and, in keeping with the Southwest spirit, was re-named the Co-Heart Program. Today, 8,000 of the 50,000+ Southwest employees previously worked for AirTran.

Training for Success

Establishing the right environment is crucial to Southwest's success at creating a culture in which employees are treated well, feel cared for, and therefore produce stellar results.

One example of a culture initiative geared toward generating a fun-LUVing attitude is Deck Parties on Monday nights. The reason—uniquely Southwest—is that on Monday evening you should celebrate the fact that the worst day of the week is over. Of course, there's a more serious reason behind it too: every Monday, about 300 new hires visit the Southwest headquarters for their induction, so the Deck Party brings them right into the heart of the culture on their first day of work. The gathering takes place on a roof deck with stunning views of the runways at Dallas Love Field, a place to dream about the possibilities of the future, and to breathe in the culture that seems to become a way of life for all Southwest employees.

And Southwest does offer a unique set of possibilities for the future. In 2014, soon after the AirTran acquisition was completed, the company established a training division called Southwest University. Until then, multiple departments had done the training. The most important training at Southwest University is known as FLY (an acronym standing for Freedom, LUV, You). On their first day of work at Southwest, all new hires are flown to Dallas, where they begin the FLY course, covering the airline's history, culture, hospitality, brand, and people. At many FLY sessions, Herb or Colleen come to talk to the new hires, as do other senior executives, such as Gary Kelly. At Southwest, caring about employees begins at the top.

Christie Owens, Director of Learning at Southwest University, says the training—especially leadership training—is geared toward teaching employees to take care of people, since she believes that when people leave, they are leaving leaders, not companies. Citing an example of a leader taking care of an employee, she mentions the time her own boss, Elizabeth Bryant, when flying another airline, gave up her own seat in business class to a much more junior colleague, and insisted on taking the junior person's economy seat. This, says Christie, was a true instance of Servant's Heart in practice.

The Boarding Re-Design: a Master Class in Community

Susie Boersma Peterson is the Director of Network Operators Control–Planning at Southwest Airlines. In 2006, she was working in airport operations at Los Angeles Airport (LAX). The airline had been getting feedback from customers who were unhappy about the boarding process. Southwest was the first airline in the US that had unreserved seating. What started happening was that people would turn up early at the gate to ensure a good seat, instead of relaxing, walking around the airport, buying stuff, et cetera, as most people do once they pass through security. While this led to faster turn-around times for Southwest planes, it also caused passenger anxiety, as well as a "cattle call" vibe around boarding, leading to a negative perception of Southwest by its own passengers and passengers on other airlines.

In response to the negative customer feedback, the marketing department suggested a re-design of the boarding process. Susie was tapped to play an operations role in it. At the first meeting, the idea of switching over to assigned seating was floated. Susie was skeptical, but wasn't vocal about her skepticism. CIO Tom Nealon sensed there was something on her mind, and asked her for a one-on-one meeting. Susie explained that she felt assigned seating might not work since it was too dramatic a change for established customers loyal to the Southwest brand. She said moving to assigned seating might imply going back on the brand promise of being different from other airlines. To her surprise and delight, Susie received the go-ahead to design a process to test alternatives on Southwest's customers and eliciting feedback. Apart from ensuring that overall customer experience improved, her mandate was fourfold: reduce customer anxiety dramatically, keep turnaround times fast, make it easy to implement, and create procedure that would help develop new ancillary revenue streams.

They tested different procedures at San Diego Airport. During and after each test-boarding, the team observed and talked to passengers. They repeated the process every week, compared responses to each procedure with the others, and reported the results. At every point of the testing, Susie remembers, she didn't want to let the customers down.

Once a month, she presented the findings to the CEO, with the CIO in tow, and gained an attentive audience. "The senior management listened to me; they listened to customers," says Susie. In effect, she was awarded ownership of the project. Ultimately, they tested five different boarding procedures. It clearly emerged that assigned seating would not work. Instead, the procedure they chose was a refinement of the previous one. While keeping seating free, and assigning groups like before, they additionally assigned boarding numbers based on how early the passenger had checked in. This eliminated the situation they'd had before where passengers crowded around the boarding gate, anxious lest their place in line be lost, unable to go shop or even take a restroom break.

Having chosen a new procedure, they then faced the challenge of implementation, especially tricky since the prior procedure had run unhindered for 30 years, and had become one of the most recognizable aspects of the Southwest brand. The marketing department led a comprehensive re-education campaign through posts on the Southwest website, a blog, and videos on screens at the boarding area.

Susie remembers with a smile that this was the fastest project ever executed at Southwest. In under nine months they designed, tested, and implemented an entirely new procedure. All the while, Tom was her internal mentor, and actively gave her feedback during weekly reviews, ensuring that her confidence and passion for the project never flagged.

The new boarding process, unveiled in the second half of 2007, epitomizes what it means to be Southwest. Always keeping customer happiness in mind, several departments collaborated on the project: Marketing came up with the insight that something needed to change; Operations put together plans for the re-design; and Customer Experience came in with IT to study how the different procedures they tested would impact turnaround times and passenger experience. The execution of the project was a master class in close community collaboration and excellence in leadership. Susie was happy to receive ownership of the project, and direct audience with the CEO and CIO, who were attentive to her concerns. Almost ten years later, what she remembers most about the intense work that went into re-designing this key operations process is how it made her *feel*.

In subsequent years, the airline continued to modify the boarding procedure with customer happiness in mind. They began offering the opportunity to purchase one of the earliest boarding positions at the gate for an additional fee, when available. They also added EarlyBird Check-In and Business Select Fare, which allocated higher numbers in the boarding queue to passengers willing to pay more for the convenience. As the airline put it: "Offering customers the option to improve their boarding position on the day of travel is one more way we can offer the travel experience that best fits their needs."

From designing the process together, to testing the process, to finalizing and marketing it, to fine-tuning it in subsequent years, Southwest employees were the stars in charge of guaranteeing that a key customer-facing process was done right. It all boils down to Southwest's simple, people-centric formula: *if we have happy employees, they will make our customers happy*. It works.

Customer Service with a Heart

The mission of Southwest Airlines is "Dedication to the highest quality of Customer Service delivered with a sense of warmth, friendliness, individual pride, and Company Spirit." It is not just a statement papered on walls and plastered on websites. It is the driving force at Southwest, where every employee learns to care about customers.

Today's generation of customers knows Southwest delivers excellent, responsive customer service on social media channels, setting it apart from many of its peers who are struggling to cope with the challenges of the digital age. For Southwest, moving their excellence to online platforms is merely a continuation of tradition.

Lisa Anderson, Director of Social Media at Southwest, has been with the company for 28 years. When we spoke with her, she recalled starting her career with American Airlines, and then paused to stifle a sob. From a relatively unknown and uncared for employee at American, Lisa became a star at Southwest. In the early 80s, she was charged with managing the transition of Southwest's customer service channel from letters to phone.

While written words offered an easy way to add quirkiness to a customer service response, telephone was more difficult. The phone conversation happened in real time and required quick thinking — and hopefully immediate resolution. Working directly with Gary Kelly and Colleen Barrett, Lisa developed the Southwest personality on the phone: fun, warm, witty, compassionate, edgy—but importantly, "not a prankster." For Lisa, setting the tone of voice at Southwest remains a crowning glory of her three decades at the airline.

Of course, phone is no longer the customer service channel of choice for Southwest's customers. But the foundations stay the same. The same personality that was once expressed over the phone can now be observed in action on Twitter and Facebook. Updated for the digital age, Southwest's customer service approach retains its core philosophy of putting customers first.

Lisa says: "How to respond is what has changed, the response itself has always been fun." Just as Mike Hafner has said that every employee has a story, so Lisa likes to say that every seat has a story. One way that Southwest embodies this belief in the digital age is via a blog that proudly displays customers' stories about why they love the airline.

Another way the airline has shown its love for its customers on social media: in August of 2012, they started offering "fan-only" tickets at a 50 percent discount, in celebration of being the first airline to get three million likes on Facebook. (This was, of course, in an age when likes were still considered significant, and not merely numbers that could be gamed or bought.) The response was huge, and the Southwest website soon started experiencing delays in processing the bookings. Soon after, the high number of booking attempts caused a glitch in which people were charged as many as 35 times for one booking.

When news of the overcharges spread, users started checking their accounts, and thousands tried reach the airline's call center. The center was not prepared to handle the high volume of calls, and distraught customers faced long delays. However, the social media team picked up the slack: they kept a close eye on both Twitter and Facebook, and publicly replied to each complaint with a solution. They often asked customers to send direct messages to receive more personalized attention.

Thanks to its social media team, Southwest Airlines managed a spectacular recovery and showed the world a few new tricks. This was one of the first times agents used their "personal-corporate" Twitter handles to reply to customers. For the first time, customers could see exactly who they were talking to, giving a human touch to the company's efforts.

Another great innovation of the social media team: they are integrated with the Network Operations Center. This enables them to have real-time knowledge of operations and update customers accordingly online. And the telephone training carries over into written communication online: staff are still trained extensively in using the correct brand voice—a delicate process that takes practice, time, and guidance. Lisa says one of the ways they train staff is by using real tweets from Southwest and its competitors, but with the airline name removed. Trainees are asked to identify which airline posted the tweets. Those who have difficulty identifying Southwest's tweets have to undergo further training.

Customer Service Becomes Hospitality

In developing Southwest's customer service philosophy, Colleen Barrett created an unusual pyramid that puts employee satisfaction at the top, then the needs of the passengers, and finally shareholders. A typical move by Colleen, during a time when fewer people were using call centers and more people were booking online, was to offer reservation clerks a chance to stay with the company rather than laying them off.

Colleen believes that the reward is the extra effort that Southwest employees put into serving passengers. In a speech at Wharton, she described how when planes were grounded across America after the September 11 attacks, a number of Southwest jets were forced to land in cities where the airline doesn't normally fly, creating some unusual dilemmas. For example, there were unaccompanied minors on some of those flights. Members of the flight crews took in the kids for the week; such a bond was created between those crews and the kids that they still keep in touch at Christmas and Thanksgiving. And in Sioux Falls, South Dakota, where one of the jets ended up after September 11, the pilot decided his passengers were watching too much television in their motel rooms, so he rented a bus to take them all out to the movies.

This kind of caring is natural at Southwest. But there are also strict service metrics to ensure that staff adheres to high standards. There is an external Net Promoter Score for customers, and there is an internal one for staff that tracks employee performance. Typically each cabin crew sees about 1500 customers a day, and each is encouraged to share stories during their flight de-briefs of how they made a difference to some customer's life.

Once every few months each top Southwest executive must serve in a customer-facing position in the field. Mike Hafner says these days help top management experience what customers are experiencing—the real product. The objective is for executives to understand what if anything is inhibiting the staff from being successful, to identify where change can happen, and to ensure that crewmembers learn from their mistakes.

Southwest goes to great pains to explain that what they truly deliver is hospitality, which is more than just customer service. Chris Robbins, a coach at Southwest Airlines University, writes: "We've always said that we're a customer service organization who just happens to fly airplanes. So what's the deal with our new focus on hospitality? And what's the difference? Are customer service and hospitality the same, or not?"

Hospitality is, as it turns out, not quite the same as customer service. It's more about being genuine and authentic. It's about helping your guest feel at home. It's about creating a relationship between the server and the served. Customer service is a set of protocols and procedures, while hospitality is a feeling.

To aid in the feeling, Southwest has developed a Hospitality Wheel. The points on the wheel are *welcome, serve, engage, appreciate, repeat.* And the strategy is paying off. According to the Department of Transportation, Southwest Airlines has consistently received among the lowest ratio of complaints per passenger of all major U.S. carriers since September 1987, when the DOT began tracking Customer Satisfaction statistics and publishing its Air Travel Consumer Report.

Indeed, even in our current age of internet-aided instant outrage, customers are as delighted with Southwest as ever. The airline receives four positive emails for every one negative. Astoundingly, Lisa says, this ratio has held steady even on Facebook, where customers are known to share poor experiences much more readily than positive ones.

More than keeping negatives low, Southwest has uniquely nurtured an avid fan base eager to stand up for Southwest when crisis strikes. In 2010, the actor and director Kevin Smith, who has a large

Twitter following, tweeted about being discriminated against and thrown off a Southwest flight for being fat. We should add that this is Smith's interpretation. Southwest management says Smith was refused travel after becoming irate that he was required to purchase a second seat as required by airline policy. In the face of a Twitter tantrum that lasted a long time, Southwest apologized publicly and tried earnestly to make it right with the actor, even putting up an official statement on its blog. While the actor rebuffed all attempts at reconciliation, Southwest's followers online stood up for the airline and tweeted in its support. What threatened to be a major PR disaster was diffused by the sheer good will of people who had benefitted from Southwest's service over the years.

And it seems that good will has prevailed. In May 2016, Kevin Smith tweeted that he was flying Southwest again after a break of six years.

"Transfarency"

Airline competition is now fierce. And passenger experience, according to multiple reports, is suffering, especially in the US. Legacy airlines, faced with stiff competition from low-cost carriers, thin profit margins, and passengers who are ever more price conscious, have been finding ways to compete on price, but this tends to come at the expense of passenger experience. They are offering more seats in economy—and therefore less legroom. The new basic economy class pares down legacy economy class to an absolutely no-frills product.

Recently, Gulliver, *The Economist*'s travel blog, lamented: "But passengers bemoaning this latest indignity have only themselves to blame. Why are the legacy airlines all emulating the likes of Spirit and Frontier, which have high rates of passenger dissatisfaction and complaints? Because those budget airlines are doing extremely well. Travelers have signaled that they are willing to suffer all sorts of discomforts and inconveniences for the sake of a lower fare. America's big airlines are simply giving them what they wished for." Now, if legacy customers want the legacy amenities they used to get for free, they have to pay for them on top of the base fare.

Southwest wasted no time in capitalizing on its difference from these legacy carriers. In October 2015, they launched a new tongue-in-cheek campaign aimed squarely at their competitors. Its mission was to educate customers about how other airlines use devious pricing to mislead them about actual fares—for instance, by quoting base fares that rise sharply by the time of purchase, and through hidden fees for baggage and other add-ons. Southwest, on the other hand, charges no fees for the first and second checked bags, no change fees, and no fee for free live TV. With just the right Southwest touch of humor, they coined a new term to describe their policy: "Transfarency."

The campaign was created by Southwest's ad agency, Austin -based GSD&M. It included a TV spot, print and digital components, as well as a dedicated microsite. The microsite leads, first, to a short video that states the mission up front: "Transfarency means we don't dream up ways to trick you into paying more. It means respect. Because we don't just fly you, we like you."

Kicking the competitive edginess up a notch, the microsite also has a section titled #FeesDontFly, in which it names and shames competitors for misleading customers about the actual cost of flying. One section lists Spirit Airlines' numerous fees—$30 to check one bag, $40 to check a second bag, $110 to change a flight, etc.— accompanied by the message, "Are you over other airlines charging you first and second checked bag fees, change fees, and what-the-heck-was-that-even-for fees? At Southwest, we do things differently." There are also fun quizzes on the microsite, including a "Fee or Fake" quiz that gives tips to help travelers avoid other carriers' sneaky fees. And there's a dedicated section called "Fee Hacker" because "If you have no other option than to fly another airline, you're going to need tips on how to outsmart their silly fees."

Finally, Transfarency posters and signs have been plastered across boarding gates at every Southwest destination—you can hardly miss them. Passengers are not just informed, but bombarded with the fact that Southwest's fares are the most transparent, and offer the most value.

Helen Limpitlaw, the Director of Brand Communications at the airline explains why Southwest's low fares and absence of hidden fees is a big deal: "Life happens and you might have to change the flight—then what? Paying $200 for change fees is not so attractive anymore. We would like to still maintain our original roots. As employees we still think of ourselves as leaders in the low-cost space."

The campaign epitomized not only Southwest's zany humor, but also its tenacity in tackling challenges head-on. It has been received positively by customers, and most of all by diehard Southwest fans. It also received wide media coverage, being picked up by media outlets such as the *Wall Street Journal*, *USA Today*, and *Fortune*, along with numerous aviation websites and blogs. Perhaps the ultimate measure of success: "Transfarency" has made it into Urban Dictionary, the go-to reference for internet-age slang.

On April 21, 2016, during the company's first-quarter earnings call, CEO Gary Kelly, true to Southwest form, began by thanking employees for the strong results: "First and foremost to our people, and the terrific service that they offer our customers every single day, I'm very proud of them. Our marketing department, in particular, has done a terrific job of distilling our message with our advertising campaign on Transfarency. The customer awareness of the low fare value that you get with Southwest is very high."

In all biographies on Southwest, it is mentioned as the first true low-cost airline, a path-breaking leader, an inspiration for many airlines to follow—and, of course, currently the world's largest low-cost carrier. Other successful low-cost airlines, from easyJet and Ryanair to

IndiGo and JetStar, have all been inspired by Southwest's model. It is perhaps, then, a fitting irony that Southwest is now regarded as being a step above the legacy airlines in both service and product. More and more customers are noticing the difference between the delightful service they get on Southwest and the rapidly devolving experience being offered by full-service carriers such as United. Above all, through the churn of time and industry evolution, Southwest has stayed true to its motto: "If it matters to you, it matters to us." That, ultimately, lies at the heart of Transfarency's appeal and success.

Navigating Customer Service in a Post-9/11 Atmosphere

In late November 2015, two separate incidents occurred at Chicago's Midway Airport in which Muslim or Arabic-speaking passengers were barred from flying Southwest. In the first, a Philadelphia pizza shop owner and his friend said they were told by a gate agent that they would not be allowed to board the plane because another passenger had overheard them speaking Arabic and was afraid to fly with them. The two friends called the police for help, and were eventually allowed on the flight.

Later the same day, six men of Middle Eastern descent asked to be seated together on another Southwest flight. Other passengers were alarmed by this, and Southwest employees removed the men from the flight.

The incidents, which were reported in major news outlets, were the result of irrational fear and suspicion after terrorist attacks earlier in the year in Paris, followed by the downing of a Russian plane over Egypt. While passenger fears are perhaps understandable, Southwest's bowing to these concerns is troubling, even though the passengers were finally accommodated in accordance with DOT guidelines.

In fact, these were not isolated events—a number of such discriminatory incidents have occurred on Southwest over the past year. In April 2016, as reported on NPR and in the New York Times, a college student who came to the United States as an Iraqi refugee was removed from a Southwest Airlines flight in California after another passenger became alarmed when she heard him speaking Arabic. That same month, according to press reports, a Muslim woman of Somali descent asked to switch seats with another passenger who had agreed to it. This action, apparently, raised the concerns of a flight attendant, who first disallowed the switch, and then, after a brief argument, asked the passenger to get off the flight.

The internet, predictably, has not reacted kindly to these incidents. Social media, especially, in recent months, has had an unusual number of posts and tweets about Southwest's apparent racial profiling of passengers. Some people have vowed never to fly Southwest again, while others have called for a boycott. This has upset a longstanding trend of near-unanimous support for Southwest, which has enjoyed many years of customer favor online.

These incidents have not happened only on Southwest. In March, a Muslim couple and their three children were asked to leave a United Airlines plane at Chicago airport after the pilot cited "safety issues." But the fact that they have happened at all at Southwest is unusual, and goes against the Southwest customer service philosophy. It should make every employee at Southwest cringe to learn that they might be thought of as being in the same league as United.

Today, 1.6 billion people use Facebook, almost a billion use WhatsApp, 800 million use Facebook Messenger, and many more millions use Instagram, Twitter, YouTube, and Snapchat. Stories are important. Personal experiences are the cornerstone of popular, shareable content on social media. Users are now inevitably afflicted with a sense of entitlement and power, knowing that social media offers them unprecedented amplification of their complaints. Sometimes, as in those cases of poor judgment with Muslim and Arabic-speaking passengers, those complaints are understandable, but as more users have joined, complaining voices have grown shriller and more powerful than ever, and can cause significant brand damage. Recent studies have suggested that one poor review online can negate the impact of four positive reviews. Given the age we're living in, a certain amount of dissatisfaction expressed online is going to befall any large company. But for an airline as heavily reliant on customer good will and word-of-mouth popularity, an aggregation of incidents such as those mentioned above can set the brand back significantly. And, putting aside the cold logic of metrics, these recent incidents are unusual for going against the Southwest spirit, which values service to customers so highly. Southwest might find that staying close to its core philosophies will ensure that it stays on the path to profitability, especially as it spreads its wings beyond the US.

In other instances, the airline has stayed right on point in their handling of customer complaints. In July 2016, Southwest experienced a massive technology outage, causing the airline to cancel nearly 2,000 flights. This resulted in a four-day stretch of chaos and customer frustration. Reportedly, over 250,000 passengers were affected. In true Southwest style, however, the service recovery was a master class: the airline reacted quickly, they didn't hesitate in saying sorry, they responded on multiple channels, and they even used live video to give a human face to their efforts to manage the crisis.

While the tech glitch is a different sort of crisis than the incidents of passengers being removed from flights, it goes to show that Southwest has the requisite processes in place to tackle any situation that might arise. What's needed is unflinching dedication to the Southwest ethos of service and LUV.

The Road Ahead

When Southwest flew its first Boeing 737s out of Dallas's Love Field in 1971, only 13 percent of the American public flew regularly. "Those 13 percent were all male, quite frankly, and they were all businessmen," remembers Colleen Barrett. "Women only flew if there was a family crisis. We have changed the way that people thought about flying." She is proud to point out that, among other things, low-fare air travel has held together couples in long-term, long-distance relationships, and helped divorced parents in far-off cities watch their children grow up.

The world today is very different. It is increasingly more troubled by religious strife and wars and terrorism, placing greater pressures on security, especially in air travel. The world is also more connected, and gaining a keener sense of human rights. Gender and racial sensitivity is increasing. Hence, there is a need to tread carefully and treat passengers with sensitivity, whether the passenger in question is an autistic child or an Arabic-speaking individual. Such attributes should not invite hate or suspicion. This is even more important in times when social media activism can cause immense brand damage through word of mouth amplification.

Now more than ever, Southwest needs to remain true to its roots. It has built a deservedly strong reputation as the airline of LUV. It needs to keep building and engendering that feeling in a world increasingly tormented by hate. In its passion for delivering service the Southwest way, perhaps Southwest Airlines will be the harbinger of love in aviation. More so because an appeal to love will be doubly significant in the US, in a climate of fear and suspicion fomented recently.

Moreover, as it expands its network beyond the US, Southwest's distinct culture and tradition will ensure it suitably differentiates itself from the legacy carriers that are already flying to the destinations in other countries to which Southwest will be introducing flights.

Ask Mike Hafner about the future and he says: "We are grown-ups now. We want to become the most loved and most flown airline in the world."

6X Analysis

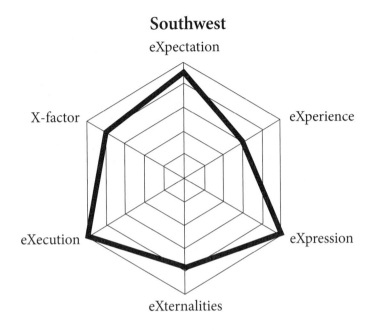

Southwest
eXpectation

X-factor

eXperience

eXecution

eXpression

eXternalities

Inspired by a strong leadership carefully cultivated by the processes Herb Kelleher and Colleen Barrett helped establish, Southwest distinguishes itself through its dedication to hospitality—a step beyond regular customer service. This is achieved by treating employees as family, based on the firm belief that good service can only happen when employees are happy and motivated. Hence Southwest's brand **eXpression** probably trumps that of most airlines around the globe—both among employees, and between employees and customers. Brand eXpression truly helps Southwest stand out from competition. This ultimately contributes to brand **X-factor** too.

The "LUV" approach has achieved great success. There are abundant heart-warming stories of Southwest's excellent service. More than anything else, this excellence is personified in their extraordinary 4:1 positive-negative customer feedback ratio—even in today's digital age where complaints are so common. The brand also differentiates itself by zany advertising that focuses on its commitment to customer happiness—as seen in their Transfarency campaign, for example. That sets the strong brand **eXpectation** that customers will be treated fairly, and differentiates Southwest from other airlines that try to nickel and dime them.

While the brand **eXperience** at Southwest, as at most low-cost airlines, remains basic, the brand **eXecution** at the airline is a standout in the field. The way the boarding process was re-designed, keeping in mind the brand tenets and the passengers' wishes, speaks volumes.

Ultimately, Southwest's unblinking adherence to core values—warrior spirit, servant's heart, fun-LUVing attitudes—has helped it become the largest domestic carrier in the US, and primed it for international success.

2: FINNAIR: DESIGNED FOR YOU

The Veteran Flight Attendant Meets the New Aircraft

On a beautiful evening in October 2015, Helena Kaartinen emerged from the forest on the edge of Helsinki-Vantaa Airport and stood by the end of the runway. A Finnair flight attendant for 36 years, Helena had not been intending to watch her company's new Airbus A350 make its first landing on Finnish soil due to her busy week. But then her 19-year-old son, an aviation geek, acted as a catalyst by saying, "Oh Mom, go for it!" And so she found herself in a crowd of more than 100 enthusiasts, eagerly waiting for the new plane to land at its new home.

Twenty minutes after Helena arrived, the A350 appeared on the horizon, glowing in the setting sun. The plane did a few loops around the airport and the crowd cheered. When we spoke with her, Helena recalled that as the plane landed, the glint of the sun off the fuselage momentarily blinded her, forcing her to close her eyes. In that moment, she thought back to her very first Finnair flight, 36 years earlier.

The year was 1979 and she was 20 years old. She'd been living at home with her parents, and was one of the youngest crewmembers on all her flights. She'd been thoroughly trained, of course, but she was also, as she put it, "a good girl," hesitant to take on the authority required to do the job effectively. She remembers, for instance, not knowing what to do when passengers older than her became drunk and unruly. But she had a few things working in her favor. For one, the older crewmembers took her under their wing. For another, the cornerstone of Finnair's service philosophy is to let employees be themselves and to give them a lot of leeway to serve passengers as they see fit. So Helena quickly grew into the job. Now, she says, she is old enough to be the mother of many of her passengers. She recognizes that when passengers on a flight get drunk, it's because something is making them anxious or uncomfortable. In her gentle maternal way, she reassures them there are other ways of relaxing than consuming a lot of alcohol, and that she will take care of them.

And now it is Helena who takes younger crew under her wing. By the time the new A350 arrived, she had already been certified as a Service Motivator for the aircraft type. It is now her job to lead her crew in Finnair's signature Nordic hospitality. As practiced by Finnair, Nordic hospitality has three components: *individuality*, *presence*, and *license to act.*

Individuality
Simply put, *individuality* is being yourself. This makes an interesting contrast with Singapore Airlines, whose Singapore Girls are trained to present a more uniform and predictable demeanor to passengers. Both airlines have an extensive network in Asia, but while Singapore Airlines gives Asian passengers the kind of deferential service more likely to be congruent with their cultural expectations, Finnair offers what Vice President of Product Development and Ancillary Jarkko Konttinen calls "a boldly distinctive customer experience."

That experience is partly comprised of the unique design elements on Finnair's planes and in their lounge, yet it is also very much comprised of their staff. Finnair's cabin crew is among the best educated of any airline in the world. Jarkko adds, "We have interesting people, including two priests who work for us!"

While Finnair flights to and from Asia always have some Asian cabin crew on board, Helena is not content to let her Asian passengers be tended to exclusively by Asian crewmembers. As she told us, "I want to take care of them myself!" We asked her if she had a service strategy for her Asian clientele and her answer typified the Finnair approach to service: "I don't have one service strategy." Rather, she tries to get a read on each individual passenger and find a way to connect, even when there is a language barrier. But she does not do this to the point of being overly insistent. She has noticed, for example, that Japanese customers tend to be less eager than others to go through the sometimes-awkward business of communicating via sign language, and she doesn't push it. But if, for example, she senses that an Indian passenger has a bit of a sense of humor, she will move her head from side to side, as many Indians do, and say "Accha!" (Hindi for "Okay!"). This usually gets a smile or a laugh, and establishes the rapport that allows the passenger to relax and entrust their flight experience to Helena. This is Helena being herself.

That, in a nutshell, is how Finnair handles the brand experience. This is not to say that the airline does nothing to create familiarity for their non-Nordic passengers. There is the aforementioned Asian flight crew. And in Helsinki-Vantaa Airport, the airline has installed signage in several Asian languages. On long-haul flights they make sure to have Asian dishes on the menu and on short-haul flights, where passengers can purchase meals à la carte from the Sky Bistro, there are also Asian options.

However, in making Helsinki the most convenient hub between Asia and Europe, and between Asia and North America, from the outset Finnair made a bold declaration: Our great strength is that we are distinctively Finnish.

Presence: Where Finnair Meets the Eye—Design

Nowhere is the uniquely Finnish identity of Finnair more evident than in its design elements both in the air and on the ground. The tagline of their advertisements is "Designed for you," which reinforces an expectation that links the airline to its meticulous, refined designs. As Finnair CEO Pekka Vauramo told us, "Design is something that we feel strongly about in this part of the world. We have very well-known designers and architects coming from Finland." Finnair has long been known for a distinctive design sensibility marked by its freshness, functionality, and simplicity. In the 1960s, the golden age of flying, Finnair teamed with the now-legendary Finnish design firm Marimekko to create uniforms for the flight attendants. And in 1969, to commemorate the occasion of the airline's first transatlantic flight to New York, they commissioned the renowned Finnish designer Tapio Wirkkala to create glassware for them. He designed a glass that was dubbed the Ultima Thule—a Latin phrase used in medieval geography to denote a place at the very limits of travel and discovery. Finnair's Ultima Thule glass evokes a melting column of ice. To this day passengers in the business-class cabin are served Finnair's signature Blue Sky cocktail of blueberry liqueur and champagne in an Ultima Thule glass.

And in the last several years Finnair has undergone a design makeover that has two main components. First, they've partnered once again with Finnish design giant Marimekko to create dishes, cutlery, textiles, and even the exterior livery of two of their airplanes. Second, the interior spaces of the new A350s, along with the business-class and premium lounges at Helsinki's airport, have been created top-to-bottom by the cutting-edge Finnish firm dSign, which made waves when it designed innovative cruise ship and hotel interiors.

Finnair and Marimekko are a particularly good fit because both have a foothold in crucial Asian markets like Japan and China. For the new collaboration, Marimekko tapped one of their lead designers, Sami Ruotsalainen, who started his design career in Japan. Ruotsalainen began by boarding a Finnair flight in summertime and looking out the window. There he encountered the main source of his inspiration: the Finnish landscape, with its four distinct seasons, its freshness, and its understated palette. Designing for the interior of a passenger aircraft comes with its own set of limitations: All objects must be smaller and lighter than their landbound counterparts. Ruotsalainen came up with a quietly stunning set of designs. He relied heavily on colors he'd seen in the landscape, dark blue for lakes and pale green for forests, as well as apple-blossom white and a stately gray. He favored the hand-drawn stripe and circle patterns that are an important part of Marimekko's repertoire. Among the objects he designed were cups, plates, teapots, cutlery, blankets, pillowcases, and aprons. He even created designs for the exterior livery of two Finnair aircraft using Marimekko's signature poppy flower with blue petals and, for a rare splash of unsubdued color, bright yellow stamens.

Passengers have been delighted by the collaboration with Marimekko. In particular, passengers from Japan, where Marimekko is already a revered and popular design brand, have enjoyed Finnair's new look. Interestingly, it is the partnership with this iconic Finnish brand that makes Finnair instantly familiar to the Japanese. Many passengers from around the globe have taken photographs of their cups and plates and posted them online on channels like Instagram. And pictures are not all they're taking—some passengers take the objects themselves! Last time we checked, a Finnair Marimekko cup was selling on eBay for $87. Jarkko Konttinen is amused by his customers' design-inspired kleptomania, which he sees as a form of marketing. He proudly reported to us that the most stolen item was the pillowcase. The Marimekko designs are a perfect embodiment of Finnair's brand identity. The freshness, the functionality, the cleanliness, and the meticulous attention to detail are all mirrored in their approach to serving their customers, and both design and service are uniquely Nordic.

The same can be said of dSign's brilliant design of Finnair's lounge and A350 cabin interiors. The relatively young design firm had already had great success in other public and private spaces, including hotels, cruise ships, shopping malls, and private homes. Led by dSign's founder, Vertti Kivi, the work for Finnair was their first for an airline. The design of the cabin and the redesign of the lounge both deploy the firm's "Space Alive" concept. Space Alive means that lighting and physical elements of the space can be altered or moved. Creating a space that is dynamic makes sense when that space is relatively small and when people are confined to it for as long as 10 hours at a time. To compensate for passengers' limited mobility, the spatial design instills a feeling of movement by playing with lights. In the cabin of the A350, the most dynamic element is the lighting. dSign's specific use of LED lights is the first on any passenger airline. The lights are installed in the ceiling, and passengers on the aircraft, even on a long flight, are treated to an evolving, nature-inspired ambient light show that evokes 24 different skyscapes, including sunrise, sunset, and different cloud formations. Cooler blues and greens tend to predominate on the northern end of flights from Finland to Asia, while on the southern end, warmer reds and oranges come to the fore. Perhaps the most dazzling lighting effect on the A350 is the Northern Lights, a subtle, shimmering dance of lights that recalls the aurora borealis above the North Pole, which can be viewed in the sky from Finnish Lapland. It gives a glimpse of the Nordic landscape to the passengers, regardless of whether Finland is their final destination.

The Finnair lounge in Helsinki also makes use of shifting ambient lighting. Curtains are used as projection screens, on which a sunrise-to-sunset sequence cycles every 20 minutes, timed in accordance with the typical duration of a passenger's stay in the lounge. Meanwhile clouds float by across the ceiling, and the modern, geometric chandeliers are lowered and raised, all contributing to the feeling that the lounge is breathing with you, and with the Finnish landscape beyond its borders.

dSign's touches of innovation and excellence are not limited to these effects of lighting and motion. The upholstery of the business-class cabin is hand-stitched. The seating configuration is 1-2-1, meaning one seat at each window and two in the center, so that flight attendants never have to reach over any passenger to serve food or drinks, give a passenger a blanket or headphones, and so on. And carry-on compartments are only above the window seats, leaving a higher-than-usual ceiling along the center of the cabin for a feeling of added spaciousness. As Chief Commercial Officer Juha Jarvinen told us, "I would say [customer feedback has been] 98 percent or 99 percent positive, and it's definitely about the feeling of spaciousness. Also the light materials and the color schemes." Indeed, TripAdvisor reviews give Finnair an overall four-star rating out of five, and reviews from passengers on the A350 consistently get a five-star rating. And women take note: The A350 comes equipped with a *ladies-only* toilet, a terrific solution to a problem that any woman who's ever stood in a long line for a public restroom can attest to. Even the flight-map visualization on the screen in front of each seat is a marvel of dynamism, with its 3D image of the globe, its satellite views, and its close-ups and long shots of the flight path.

The airline's uniquely Finnish approach to design—and brand experience—come together in these distinctive design elements. A passenger review on TripAdvisor states, "Finnair uses A350 aircraft on the long-haul leg which are very modern and equal to the A380 without the payload. The service on board is up there with other business-class airlines and the crew are very helpful with any issues." Passengers cannot help but feel that their comfort and aesthetic pleasure have been thought of in great detail by Finnair.

Unique Position in the Asian Market

Having a unique and outstanding visual identity has served Finnair particularly well in Asia because, in a very real sense, design is an international language that transcends spoken and written words. Other airlines have faltered when it comes to perception in Asia. KLM Royal Dutch Airlines, for instance, eventually realized that their blue logo topped by a crown was so similar to that of Parmalat milk that many Chinese people mistook KLM for a brand of milk. So having a strongly Nordic visual identity that is easily legible across cultures has helped Finnair create strong brand recognition in Asia, which is crucial since flights to and from Asian destinations comprise 80 percent of the airline's long-haul business, and up to 90 percent of it in the winter months.

Finnair's branding success in Asia extends well beyond design. Two elements of this success are simply facts of the airline's existence, which they've made the most of. One is their longevity. Jarkko Konttinen confesses that he hates the term "legacy"—he prefers to think of Finnair as a scrappy little boutique airline competing against the big guys in a tough market—but the fact is that Finnair was started in 1923, and age tends to garner respect in Asia. The airline has had flights to Tokyo for more than 30 years, and 25 years ago they were the first European airline to fly to Beijing. So being the elder statesman confers credibility upon Finnair.

This credibility is amplified by another sheer fact of the airline's existence–their geographical location. Jarkko says, "I mean look at the Finnish winter conditions. We're not exactly departing from under the palm trees here. So a lot of excellence has been built into

Finnair through the rough conditions, being located here on the top of the world, so to say. And this has formed the very foundation of our competitive advantage: operational excellence, safety, and reliability." This is something that allows Finnair to handle externalities better than other airlines.

Flight attendant Helena Kaartinen corroborates this. In addition to being a reassuring maternal presence on her flights, she has stone-cold knowledge of flight safety protocols for each aircraft. As she said when we were discussing her role as Service Motivator on the new A350, "The first element of training is safety. I have to have it inside me so you don't have to see it. When something goes wrong, I know what to do. You can relax and rely on me." Finnair might consider asking Helena to moonlight as a copywriter. "You can relax and rely on me" is a pretty darn good motto for any airline and especially Finnair.

In addition to operational excellence, reliability, and safety, Finland's geographical location "at the top of the world" confers upon the airline another significant advantage among Asian travelers: Helsinki's perfect position as a hub. This holds true for flights between Asia and Europe as well as Asia and North America. Finland's capital city is on a direct line from Delhi to the United States, and from Northeast Asia to Western Europe. This, of course, shortens flying time compared to other one-stop flights on the Middle East carriers or even other European ones. And to make Helsinki even more appealing as a hub, Finnair has been developing a plan in cooperation with local hotels and tour operators to invite Asian passengers to stop in Helsinki for a day or two as a cure for jet lag.

CEO Pekka Vauramo points out an added virtue of providing the shorter route from Asia to Europe and the United States: "The shorter you fly, the less fuel you burn, the less emissions you produce." Finnair's Asian flights produce up to 20 percent fewer carbon emissions than comparable flights on KLM and Lufthansa.

The Asia strategy has continued to work very well for the airline. In 2010 Finnair launched a print advertising campaign in Japan called "Mr. Europe," featuring one of Japan's most popular film actors, Koji Yakusho, and emphasizing the speed and convenience of Finnair flights from Japan to Europe. The ad won a prestigious Nikkei Advertising Award. Not coincidentally, for the first time in its history, in 2010 Finnair's ticket sales in Japan exceeded those in Finland in peak Japanese travel months.

In China, Finnair maintains constant presence on the Chinese voice and text-messaging app WeChat as well as on social network Weibo, on which it has 55,000 followers. The airline serves not only big cosmopolitan cities like Beijing and Shanghai, but secondary destinations including Chongqing, Guangzhou, and Xi'an. Helena tells us that many of the passengers from these smaller Chinese cities are first-time fliers, and she is particularly eager to take care of them. She describes a group of older women from Chongqing, off to see Europe for the first time. She said they were ebullient, laughing and joking with her despite the language barrier. And she was able to offer them useful advice about their destinations. ("Don't carry cash in Rome, you will be pickpocketed!")

Innovative Marketing without a Massive Budget

As in design and service, Finnair takes an individualistic approach to marketing. The airline's market share in Asia is five percent, and as Jarkko said, "Our marketing budgets are relatively small … so that means targeting is the key. We don't have the money to sponsor the Olympic Games."

Of course the designs by Marimekko and dSign are so distinctive and memorable that they function as their own marketing elements, particularly when passengers post photos of them on Facebook, and post the items themselves on eBay. But Finnair has come up with other innovative approaches to targeted marketing.

A particularly fun one was the Arto Saari Invitational skateboarding event at Helsinki Airport—aka, "A Match Made in HEL"—which took place over two days in October of 2014 and was documented in a video that has received nearly a quarter of a million views on YouTube. Saari, an award-winning Finnish skateboarder, invited other world-class skateboarders from Japan, the United States, Denmark, Russia, and Finland to come and skate at Helsinki Airport for two days. More than one of the skaters remarked that they'd always wanted to skate in an airport but had never been allowed. They skated on every imaginable surface: runways, hangars, stairs, ramps, along the top of a fuel truck, up and down a blast wall, down the hallways of the terminals, even on a baggage conveyor belt. The resulting video is beautiful, and the tagline is "Whatever your passion, wherever it takes you, we're the shortest way there."

"A Match Made in HEL" is not the only instance when Finnair has created a small, exciting local event and then blasted it around the world on video. On January 26, 2014, India's 54th Republic Day—the day the nation became independent—the passengers on a flight from Helsinki to Delhi were treated to a wonderful surprise: the entire flight crew, dressed in traditional Indian garb, danced Bollywood-style up and down the aisles to the Indian pop song "Om Shanti Om." The dozens of mostly European crewmembers sashaying through the aisles in their best imitation of Bollywood dancers is a charming sight to behold. From the looks of the video, both passengers and crew had a great time, and the video has had nearly six million views on YouTube.

Perhaps what is most remarkable about this event is that the idea for it came from the crewmembers themselves. They just wanted to honor their Indian passengers and treat everyone on board to some lively antics. Remember that Finnair's three core elements of Nordic hospitality are individuality, presence, and *license to act*. The crew-led Republic Day dance was a noteworthy instance of *license to act*.

The Republic Day event also set the stage for another Bollywood-related extravaganza spearheaded by Helena Kaartinen. It began when she had layovers in Delhi and Mumbai (the airline no longer flies to Mumbai but still has service to Delhi). As Helena said, "I got India growing in me. I needed to know more and more and more." Eventually she took a holiday to India, and found herself becoming increasingly curious about the infamous slums in Mumbai.

Finally she met a man named Ashley Pereira, who did charity work in a slum neighborhood called Saki Naka Pipeline, and he took her there. Helena and Ashley were joined by fellow Finnair flight attendant Manish Gawde. They were particularly charmed by the children they met. One little girl spontaneously recited a poem for them. Helena and Manish cooked up a plan to do something special for the kids.

As it turned out, before joining Finnair, Manish had been a Bollywood dance instructor, and the two flight attendants hatched a plan to create a Bollywood dance video featuring kids from Saki Naka, which they dubbed "Flight of Fantasy." They held auditions, and then set up a training camp for the kids to learn the dance. On the appointed day, the kids' parents brought them by bus to the airport for a flight to New Delhi, where the filming of the dance would take place. It was a very emotional moment for the parents—none of their kids had ever been on an airplane before. As for the kids, Helena said, "They were screaming when the plane took off, 'Aaaah!' like they were on a roller coaster or something." When they got to Delhi, they performed the dance in Finnair flight attendant uniforms on the rooftop of a hotel, and that, too, has been uploaded to YouTube, along with a video that tells the story of how "Flight of Fantasy" came to be.

Here again we encounter the third of the three key service elements of Finnair: *license to act*. The idea for "Flight of Fantasy" came entirely from Helena and Manish. When Helena presented it to Finnair management—with a budget for the flight, the uniforms for the kids, the film crew, and so on—she got a quick yes. Airline management encourages flight attendants and other staff to take initiative, even when that initiative, like "Flight of Fantasy," goes well beyond the conventional ways of serving customers. This project was a win-win: Finnair got a wonderful marketing product for a key Asian market like India, and the kids from Saki Naka got an experience they'll remember for the rest of their lives.

The Future

As the airline looks ahead, they are focused on expanding upon their strengths. More good design is coming down the pike, of course. As Juha Jarvinen told us, the great success of Vertti Kivi's interior design of the A350 has the airline gearing up for a renewal of the rest of the fleet—both the wide-body and narrow-body aircraft. They also have plans in the near future to expand the terminal at Helsinki-Vantaa Airport. They opened a premium lounge, and are possibly also looking at building a working lounge to accommodate fliers who do not qualify for the business-class or premium lounges. In this way the airline will continue to enhance the brand experience through one of their standout strengths, Finnish design.

They are also looking for ways to continue increasing brand visibility in Asia. While they welcome all travelers, they are focusing especially on seasoned travelers. As Head of Marketing Communications Emmi Teras puts it, "If it's your first time going to Europe, you are likely to select a local carrier. But if you have experience traveling between Europe and Asia … you are more educated about what you want from a service … and you may be exploring other cities than only Paris." So the airline is placing a lot of emphasis on expanding brand recognition among experienced travelers by marketing Finnair as a viable alternative to local airlines.

There is an ongoing learning curve in their Asian marketing.

The Finnair marketing team is continually trying to advance their knowledge about what messages gain traction in the various languages and cultures. Sometimes the difference between what works and what doesn't is very subtle, and they've been seeking a lot of customer feedback to help them refine their message. For example, as former Marketing Consultant in the Global Brand department, Olli Lehtonen, told us, they tried marketing Finnair as the shortcut between Europe and Japan. The response from Japanese customers was head scratching. "They're like 'What's the shortcut?'" But when they simplified the message to "Finnair is the fastest airline," the Japanese customers immediately got the point. They tried a message, it didn't quite work, they listened carefully to their customers' responses, they modified the message, and on the second try, the message hit its mark. This strikes us as a lesson for any global brand in how to communicate effectively across cultures.

To be able to strike a chord as a brand with Asians on a sustained basis, Finnair would do well to set up marketing and customer research teams based in the regions most important to their business. Ultimately, hiring Shanghainese staff in an office in Shanghai to create brand messages targeted to local businessmen would reap strong results that would be difficult to achieve for a team of Europeans in Helsinki.

6X Analysis

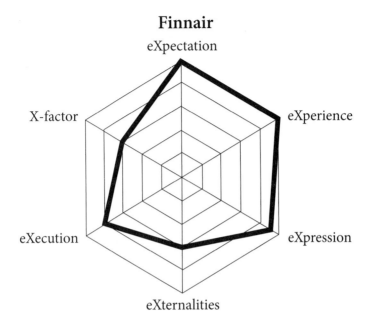

Finnair

eXpectation

X-factor

eXperience

eXecution

eXpression

eXternalities

Finnair differentiates itself by offering a unique design-focused brand identity; a reliable, yet individualistic approach to service; and by offering passengers in Asia an easy bridge to Europe and the United States.

Through partnerships with legendary designers such as Marimekko (for cutlery and textiles), and recent partnerships with dSign (for the A350 and business-class lounge interiors) that improve passenger experience through design, Finnair continues to cultivate a distinctive brand **eXperience**.

Despite being one of the oldest airlines in the world, Finnair enjoys promoting itself as an underdog, which can be seen in its zany advertising campaigns and smart targeted outreach in important markets. The airline also carefully designs the on-board experience that offers a local Nordic flavor without alienating passengers from different cultures. This ensures that the brand **eXpectation** is intricately maintained.

In addition, Finnair employees—and crew, especially—enjoy a *license to act* that ensures passengers are taken care of at every stage of the journey. For an airline that combines multiple elements in a delicate balance—distinctive design, endearing individuality, a sense of comfort—Finnair has truly managed to master the art of brand **eXpression**.

Note: If you would like to see what the Finnair A350 experience was like, drop me an email at finnairA350@simpliflying.com and I'll be happy to send you the photos and videos from the flight.

3: AIRASIA: NEVER SAY NEVER

From Music to Aviation: the Journey of an Airline Rock Star

The story of the remarkable rise of AirAsia from a debt-ridden state-owned airline with a two-plane fleet to the number one low-cost commercial carrier in Asia is ultimately the story of the people who made it happen.

First and foremost is Tan Sri Anthony Francis Fernandes, aka Tony Fernandes, the co-founder and Rock Star in Chief of AirAsia, and the brand's ultimate champion and **X-Factor**. Fernandes was born in 1964 and grew up in Malacca, a town on the west coast of peninsular Malaysia. His mother was an entrepreneur and his father was a physician who worked for the World Health Organization. At the age of six, Fernandes began playing piano at his mother's Tupperware parties and singing songs she'd written about her product. As Fernandes told *Forbes* recently, "My mother could sell ice to an Eskimo, and so she had a phenomenal business." Fernandes traveled around Malaysia with her, and through this experience he became familiar both with commercial aviation and with how to successfully market a product.

At twelve he went to boarding school at Epsom College in England. While his British classmates went home for the holidays, the high cost of air travel to Malaysia at the time left him unable to leave England, so he spent his holidays in London, with frequent trips to Heathrow Airport. "I was a bit of a plane spotter. My friends and I used to stand on top of the Queen's Building, Car Park 2, and just watch planes land. Ages 13 to 17. Very sad, really, but… it was better than spotting trains, I suppose."

Not long after graduating from the London School of Economics with a degree in accounting, he started working in the music business in London. He was the financial controller for Virgin Communications, whose CEO, Richard Branson, knows a thing or two about starting an airline after having success in the music business. Fernandes eventually became the Vice President of Warner Music in Southeast Asia. He left in 2001, when the company announced its merger with America Online. That same year he came to an agreement with the Malaysian government to pay them the symbolic sum of one Ringgit for AirAsia, which had $40 million of debt at the time.

The story of how he transformed the airline into the number one low-cost carrier in Asia is the story of his unique leadership style and his unconventional methods. Among his first unconventional moves was to hire a lot of people from outside the airline business, a practice he continues to this day. As he told us when we spoke to him, "You need aviation insiders to fly the plane and fix the plane, but apart from that I wanted to have fresh thought and different perspective." And he meant it: from the very beginning, Fernandes has trusted and encouraged his staff to bring fresh ideas to him and execute them as they saw fit.

One of his earliest hires was a trusted marketing colleague from the music business, Joyce Lai, who was up for the challenge of making the leap from music to aviation, as Tony had done. In some ways she had to start from scratch. "In music we had all these journalist relationships," she told us, "but we didn't know anybody on the business desks…. We had to start all over again, and so the traditional way back then was to check out all the newspapers and see who was the editor and start building your database."

However, in launching an airline, she was also able to transfer over a lot of the skills and concepts she used to launch a new musician. "We looked at Tony like a breaking artist, and we said, you know what, we just have to make a superstar out of him, and how do you do that?" Luckily they were working with a man who had a personality that was both charming and forceful. (Tony, who has now become good friends with Richard Branson, once made a bet with his former Virgin Music boss on a Formula One race. The loser had to dress up as a female flight attendant and serve passengers on the other's airline. Branson lost, and duly dressed in drag on an AirAsia flight from Perth, Australia, to Kuala Lumpur, where Tony made the following announcement: "He is an entrepreneur, visionary, knight, and adventurer. Sir Richard can now also add AirAsia flight attendant to his long list of credentials.")

One simple but memorable thing they did early on was to have him wear a red baseball cap with the AirAsia logo whenever he was out in public. Before long, Tony could hardly walk through an airport without being mobbed by fans who wanted him to pose for a photo with them, as if he really were a hit recording artist.

Joyce said the airline actually began with a lot of strengths: in addition to Tony, they had great pilots and cabin crew, and because they were offering such low fares, which had not really been done before in Asia, they had all kinds of people flying with them who'd never flown before. They had a fun and funky brand. But they had to be careful with that, marketing-wise. As Joyce put it, "Can you imagine, low cost, fun, funky? It would be like, my gosh, is this an airline, or what?" So again, she drew upon her experience in marketing musicians: "In the music business, we say go out with one single at a time, and make it work, and then follow up with a second, third, fourth single. Then you have a fantastic album. And then at some point in your career you have a Greatest Hits album. So if Tony Fernandes was the artist, his first single was "low fares." The airline's slogan, "Now everyone can fly," was the catchiest line of the song. Today, with flights to over 120 destinations in 24 countries, it would be fair to say the airline has reached the Greatest Hits stage of success.

Joyce makes an interesting point about defining the brand with regard to using the term "low fares" when the industry term "low cost" would have been the more obvious way to go: "'Low cost tends to put a different kind of perception into minds.'" Even though AirAsia had one of the highest safety ratings from the Department of Civil Aviation, "People initially thought, 'Oh my God, are your pilots trained?'" So the term "low fares" helped ease passengers' minds that the airline was delivering affordable travel without cutting corners where it mattered.

Once they began to establish the airline with Tony Fernandes as its figurehead, and "low fares" as its core strength, then they could begin to feature other elements to build out the brand: their exceptional service, their pilots, their crew, and the growing number of passengers who were their strong supporters.

Believe the Unbelievable, Dream the Impossible, and Don't Take No for an Answer

Meanwhile, starting a low-cost airline presented substantial challenges. One of Tony's cost-saving initiatives, which remains in effect to this day, was the 25-minute turnaround, meaning that between the time an aircraft arrives at the gate and the time it departs, no more than 25 minutes goes by. By comparison, typical turnaround time for full-service airlines is anywhere from 45 to 120 minutes. One obvious way to reduce turnaround time—and to save costs—was to offer no meal service, eliminating both the load-in of new meals for each flight and the additional cleanup required after a flight with meal service. This has now evolved into an on-demand meal service, where a majority of meals are pre-ordered during the booking process on the AirAsia website. This way, hardly any food is wasted and little extra weight needs to be carried on board the aircraft.

The biggest challenge of the quick turnaround, however, had to do with airline personnel. In order to keep costs down and make the 25-minute turnaround work, Tony did not hire a clean-up crew but called on the cabin crew to do the cleanup. Captain Chin Nyok San, who was then AirAsia's head of operations, was concerned about asking pilots and crew to go above and beyond what was usually expected of airline personnel in those positions, so he went to Tony with an unusual request. There had recently been a bird strike at Kuala Lumpur International Airport that resulted in planes being grounded for half a month. Captain Chin asked Tony if he would pay his pilots for that time, even though they were not flying. The captain told us, "He kept quiet, but after three days he said yes." Not only did Tony's reasonableness motivate pilots and crew to take on the extra duties during turnaround, but as Captain Chin said, "He gained the trust of most of the senior guys in the company, and that is why… most of the pilots, engineers, and the senior cabin crew are still with us today."

The quick turnaround enabled AirAsia to operate its planes for an average of about 13 hours a day, as compared with the typical 10.5 hours a day for full-service carriers. This and other measures reduced the airline's costs by 13 percent in its first year under Fernandes' leadership.

Still, there were bigger hurdles ahead. Fernandes' goal was to provide service to all ten countries in the Association of Southeast Asian Nations (ASEAN), but he encountered a lot of resistance from some of the countries' regulatory agencies. The most intense resistance came from Singapore. Tony made repeated efforts to secure permission to fly his planes to Singapore's Changi Airport directly from Kuala Lumpur. In 2004, he went so far as to schedule a flight from Kuala Lumpur to Johor Bahru, Malaysia, a town just across the straits from Singapore. He then put passengers on a bus for the remaining 100 or so kilometers to get them across the border. The government of Singapore caught wind of Tony's workaround and impounded the buses the moment they entered Singapore!

But this did not stop Tony. According to Yap Mun Ching, who was the airline's route manager at the time and now runs the AirAsia Foundation, it took six years of lobbying the Singapore government to relent and allow AirAsia to land at Changi. This is a great example of how Tony's persistence and can-do attitude has helped the airline to triumph over hard times. As Tony told us, "I remember a reporter saying to me, 'Don't you get tired of fighting this? Because I am tired of reporting it.' But… how can we call ourselves ASEAN if we don't have a flight to Singapore?" When we asked him how he finally succeeded, he said, "Just keep pushing and lots of publicity, lots of press. And you know it irritated a lot of people, but Nelson Mandela did a lot more than I've ever done, so if he can do it, we can do it."

Interestingly, when AirAsia finally started direct flights from Singapore, they held a press conference in a room with the Singapore Airlines headquarters visible in the background, and placed a banner in front of it that had a photo of an AirAsia flight attendant and said, "There's a new girl in town. Twice the fun. Half the price." The same advertisement taking a dig at the Singapore Girl was plastered across billboards in Singapore and drove lots of publicity for the airline.

Fernandes' mantra, not just for himself but for his employees as well, has been "Believe the unbelievable, dream the impossible, and don't take no for an answer." We were struck by how many of the AirAsia personnel we spoke with had their own don't-take-no-for-an-answer stories, inspired by their boss. Perhaps the story to beat all stories in that vein is that of Kugan Tangiisuran, who joined AirAsia in 2005 as a 17-year-old dispatch boy in the HR department. He told us that he had only one reason for getting a job at the airline: to become a pilot. Dispatch boy, a clerical job, was what was available at the time he applied, so he took it. The airline had a policy of not allowing new employees to change departments for the first two years, but as soon as his two years were up, he took the exam to qualify for being a pilot. And he failed. The exam has Math, English, and Physics portions, and Kugan's knowledge of physics at the time was not sufficient to get him through the test. He tried the exams two more times and failed again, twice more.

One of the interesting things about AirAsia is that it has what Tony refers to as a flat structure with regard to employees, meaning that hierarchy is downplayed, everyone can contribute ideas, and everyone can talk to everyone. By 2009, Kugan was working as a dispatch boy in the CEO's office and saw Tony frequently. He told his CEO about his aspirations, and his failures. Tony told him it would probably be a good idea for him to go and study physics, and repeatedly encouraged him not to give up.

In 2011, Kugan had still not succeeded in getting into the cadet shift, the program for training pilots, and was still in his clerical job. One of his bosses said to him, "Why do you still want to be a dispatch boy?" and offered him a job as a flight attendant. He turned it down, because despite his failures thus far, he was still gunning for the pilot job. In 2013 one of the field captains offered Kugan a tour of the cockpit, and Kugan even turned *that* down, "because I wanted to go in as a pilot."

Finally, in 2014, after eleven tries—*eleven tries!* Kugan passed the pilots' exam, aced the subsequent interviews, and was admitted to cadet pilot training. In May of 2015 he made his first non-simulated flight, and in August of that year he piloted his first commercial flight with passengers on board.

Tony Fernandes came to Kugan's graduation ceremony, beaming like a proud father. He gave a speech making a special note of his new pilot's extraordinary accomplishment. "He never gave up, and I never allowed him to give up. I kept saying, 'Don't give up.' I don't want quitters. I want people who believe in their ability, and can go out there and be the best." Fighting back tears, Tony added, "In my 15 years, I've had so many fantastic stories, but nothing makes me prouder than to see a young man like Kugan, who never gave up."

Empowering Employees

Over and over again, the AirAsia personnel we spoke to told us stories about how Tony empowered them to do their jobs as they saw fit. Yap Mun Ching is a case in point. Before joining AirAsia as a route planner she was a political journalist. The Malaysian laws governing print journalism were very restrictive, but in the 1990s, when she began her career, internet journalism was a burgeoning field, and as an online reporter she had much more freedom to cover the stories that interested her. She thought Tony Fernandes was an interesting guy who kept running into politicians, so she arranged an interview with him. In the interview she asked him why one of AirAsia's very first international destinations was Bandung, Indonesia, which was not a hub by any stretch. "He sort of hesitated, and then he said 'I used to make music videos there, it's a beautiful place.' That got him thinking how he [chose his routes]. He did things very instinctively."

Tony then turned the interview around and began asking Yap Mun Ching questions. Where had she gone to school? (In England, like Tony; they bonded over their mutual interest in easyJet, the British low-cost carrier.) What had she studied? (Economics.) By the end of the interview Tony offered her the job of route planner for

AirAsia. She was about to leave for a three-month press fellowship in Cambridge, and, as Yap Mun Ching recalls it, "He said, 'Okay, just come back after three months and send me your c.v. and we will see." Three months later, at age 27, with no prior experience, she became a route planner for AirAsia.

When she arrived at her new job, her new job didn't really exist. AirAsia did not have a route planning division. She was put in the route revenue division, and, as she said, her boss in route revenue "set me some tasks which I felt were quite boring. Tony used to walk around the office quite a lot, so he said 'Hi, how are you?' and I said, 'I am really bored.' He was kind of taken aback, and then he said, 'No, it gets better, you just have to be patient.' Three weeks later he came back again and he said, 'So how is it now?' and I said, 'I'm still bored.'.... Then he gave me a challenge. He said, 'Okay, we are getting a new aircraft in three weeks. Write me a report about where you think it should fly.'" She sent him the report, he approved it, and that is how the ex-journalist and her new boss created her new job at AirAsia.

The more success Yap Mun Ching had, the more responsibility Tony gave her. Not long after she arrived, the airline transitioned its fleet from Boeing 737s to Airbus 320s. Yap Mun Ching told us Tony approached her one day and said, "'We bought these aircraft. Can you figure out how we do the transition?' So I asked him, 'What do you want me to look at?' and he said, 'You've just got to figure it out.'" She had eight months to do it, a very short amount of time for a transition of that magnitude that involved phasing in a new aircraft fleet.

Just as Joyce Lai brought her experience marketing music to her new job in the airline business, Yap Mun Ching told us she drew upon her skills as a journalist when she was figuring out the fleet transition. "It was really about interviewing people. I talked to the chief engineer, the chief pilot, all these guys, finding out what their individual needs were. Nobody at any point told me 'This is how it's done at this airline.'" She had the complete backing of Tony, who had made it clear to the senior people that yes, he was putting a 27-year-old with no aviation experience in charge of the transition, because he trusted her. And since Tony had earned the trust of the chief engineer et al, they cooperated, and Yap Mun Ching succeeded. It is typical of Tony's leadership style to entrust his people with enormous tasks that will have major consequences for the business, whether or not those people have aviation experience.

She put her journalist's skills to use in other aspects of her job as well. As she said, "When you interview someone… you have to put yourself in that person's shoes to see what they have to face. So every time we went to an airport and made a pitch… we thought of it in terms of what would benefit them, and then we sold it to them in their language." A case in point is Shenzhen, China. AirAsia had already made the decision that it was too difficult to start with the major Chinese hubs, so they began their service to China by flying to the southern city of Macau. Once they had eleven flights a day to Macau, they were approached by Shenzhen. "You have to understand what each of these airports has," she said. "Shenzhen is an airport trapped between Hong Kong and Guangzhou. They are not a capital city but they are not Hong Kong either…. So we looked at it as, 'You will never be bigger than these guys, but we can feed you because we won't fly to Hong Kong, we won't fly to Beijing.'" The head official at Chongqing told her that his airport was plenty big, that it was used by 20 million passengers a year. Again, using her journalist's instincts, she realized that the issue for this man was not money but prestige. So, appealing to this, she told him if he wanted to be a truly important airport he would need international flights, whereas at the time Shenzhen mostly had domestic flights. She also promised flights would begin within three months, and that there would be three flights a day within a year, if Shenzhen officials would lobby Beijing for the necessary permits. And so the psychological tactics of the journalist helped the airline route planner gain a foothold in China.

Captain Chin also exemplifies Tony's philosophy of trusting and empowering his employees. Perhaps even more consequential than the captain's request that Tony pay his pilots and crew for the half a month they were grounded during the bird strike was his decision in 2003 to purchase six flight simulators when the airline needed only two. Captain Chin's reasoning was this: AirAsia pilots had to travel overseas to do their training on a simulator; that was true not only for AirAsia, but for every airline in the region; air travel in Southeast Asia was booming, so there was high demand for new pilots, and therefore also for simulators; so AirAsia could use the two simulators they needed to train their own pilots, and lease out the other four to other airlines, thus covering the cost of the purchase. When the captain brought this proposal to Tony, his response was not "Please present me with a detailed cost/benefit analysis for this purchase." It was simply, "Are you sure?" Captain Chin's answer was yes, he made the purchase, and sure enough he was right: it has turned into a very good investment for the airline, as initially the additional simulators were leased, and later fully utilized to support AirAsia's own growth.

Even the AirAsia cabin crew have the leeway to handle things as they see fit. Despite being an Asian airline, AirAsia's cabin crew resembles that of European and American airlines like Finnair and Southwest at least as much as they resemble a more traditionally Asian crew like Singapore Airlines. For example, while Singapore enforces strict guidelines about how flight attendants must wear their hair, AirAsia crew are encouraged to wear their hair as they wish to. And they are given autonomy as to how to handle any situations that may arise during a flight.

As Group Head of Cabin Crew Suhaila Hassan told us, there is of course some level of uniformity in the AirAsia crew's treatment of passengers. For example, the passenger greeting that Tony has instituted is a traditional Indonesian greeting: palms together in front of the chest and a slight bow. But even within the uniformity, there is a sense of empowerment akin to that of Finnair's crew: AirAsia flight attendants refer to the people they're serving not as passengers, but as guests. This shift in vocabulary signals an increase in responsibility on the part of the crew. As Suhaila told us, "When someone comes to our home, of course we want to give them the best, right?"

The more relaxed standards for AirAsia crew's individuality combined with the high standards for how they treat the airline's guests have resulted in top-notch service. At the World Travel Awards in 2015, AirAsia's flight attendants were honored as Asia's Leading Cabin Crew, beating out not only other low-cost carriers, but even full-service carriers such as Singapore Airlines, famous for their world class service standards.

2014: The Crash

On December 28, 2014, AirAsia Flight QZ 8501 from Surabaya, Indonesia, to Singapore, crashed into the Java Sea, killing all 155 passengers and seven crew. A fatal accident is of course the worst **eXternality** an airline can face, and Tony took it very much to heart. His way of handling the tragedy demonstrated once again his unusual capacity for leadership.

He recognized that there were two groups of grief-stricken people in this situation: the families and loved ones of the passengers, and the families, loved ones, and colleagues of the crew. Within hours of the flight's disappearance from the radar he was in Surabaya meeting with families of both groups. For those family members who were arriving from out of town, the airline immediately set up transportation and accommodations. They also issued regular statements in multiple languages detailing what they knew about the crash, and set up a hotline for relatives.

Tony communicated not only face to face, but through as many channels as he could. In a televised news conference, he said, "I apologize profusely for what they are going through. I am the leader of this company and I take full responsibility." He also tweeted to his staff: "I as your Group CEO will be there through these hard times. We will go through this terrible ordeal together and I will try to see as many of you." Tony shared with us that it "was the most horrific time of [his] life."

Of course family members were devastated, but still many were grateful for the way the airline treated them. "AirAsia has taken good care of us from day one," said the uncle of one deceased passenger. As much as anything else, people were consoled by Tony's presence, and his taking full responsibility for the crash and being personally involved. Tragedy is a true test of leadership and Tony handled this aviation disaster with the gravitas befitting a leader of his stature, in the process re-writing the rule book on airline crisis communications.

An Airline for Ordinary People, by Ordinary People

That Tony was immediately on the scene and speaking face to face with people affected by the crash is in keeping with his core values, with which he has imbued the airline. Tony's mother may have influenced him to become an entrepreneur, but it was likely his father, a doctor who believed medical treatment should be available to everyone for free, who influenced him to create an airline for ordinary people. The company estimates that up to half its passengers are first-time fliers. "If I want to get a high," Tony told *Forbes*, "I just walk down to the terminal and see the numbers of people who want to take photographs with me. It's not the vanity part. It's that we have genuinely changed people's lives by allowing them to travel. Regularly, an old man will come up to me and say, 'I never thought I would be in a plane before I died, but now I can be.'"

In 2007, Tony leveraged the popularity of the airline to launch Tune Hotels, whose tagline is "five-star beds at one-star prices." The hotel buildings are painted in bright red and white stripes to match AirAsia's fleet of planes. The two dozen hotels now serve passengers in Malaysia, Indonesia, England, Australia, and India.

And in 2010, Yap Mun Ching, having left her position as route planner, approached Tony and asked him to contribute seed money to an organization she wanted to launch to invest in social enterprise in the region. Tony's response was yes, but let's go bigger. He'd always wanted to invest in social enterprise but had been too busy running the airline, so he suggested they create the AirAsia Foundation, and put the airlines's considerable resources behind it. In typical Tony fashion, he handed the reins to Yap Mun Ching: "So basically he just left it to me, same as before: 'You will have to figure out how you want to structure this, write the board paper, go set up the company, go register it, set up the bank accounts, pick your own trustees.'"

The foundation now invests in small businesses that have a core social component. As the foundation's website says, "From creating jobs for the underprivileged to improving animal welfare, our grantees have all strived in their own ways to make a difference." For example, they have funded a company called Sapanapro, which operates in the mountains of northern Vietnam. There is a booming tourist industry in the area that local ethnic minorities have been largely left out of, and they have had few viable ways of sustaining themselves. Sapanapro helps them commercialize local therapeutic herbs and herbal therapies sought after by tourists, thereby supporting the locals in environmentally sustainable enterprise.

Another recipient of funding has been Selaka Kotagede, which has been revitalizing the traditional silversmith trade in the Kotagede neighborhood of Yogyakarta, Indonesia. A tough economy, changing tastes in jewelry, and mass production have pushed the Kotagede silversmiths into hard times. Selaka Kotagede has been training them in new skills, introducing them to contemporary design trends, and facilitating partnerships and collectives among individual silversmiths that enable them to compete with mass producers on cost and marketing. Yap Mun Ching's approach to recruiting board members was similar to AirAsia's unorthodox hiring practices. "Most foundations will get a retired public figure to sit on their board. The idea we had was, instead of that, why don't we identify people who are on their way up, who are younger, who fit with our profile. So we looked at people in their early 40s or late 30s who can connect with our brand, who use social media, and so on." One of her choices, for instance, was the chief strategist of the Thai stock exchange, but the day he met with Yap Mun Ching, he told her he'd just resigned from the stock exchange, and questioned whether he'd be the kind of trustee she needed. She took the long view: he'd gotten a PhD in Economics from Harvard at 24, he came back to Thailand after the Asian financial crisis and helped restructure the economy. So she wasn't daunted by the fact that he was currently jobless. She turns out to have been right: a year later, after serving on AirAsia Foundation's board and doing other philanthropic activities, he became Governor of the Central Bank of Thailand.

AirAsia Foundation does not operate like a venture capital firm—they are not looking for a return on their investment. Rather, they want enterprises to use their funding in a way that will generate still more funds, so they can become self-sustaining. They recognize that eight out of ten small businesses fail, so they are not looking for an unrealistic success rate in the projects they fund. "Even if one out of ten succeeds and becomes sustainable in addressing our social environmental mission, that's a huge win for us." The foundation is yet another way the AirAsia brand looks after the little guys, the ones full-service airlines tend to overlook.

Being a democratizer in Asia is a central part of AirAsia's brand. "Generally," Tony told us, "Asia is about being the biggest, the best, the swankiest, the tallest, the richest. It's like, [expletive], I have a restaurant on the 73,000th floor and 17 Gucci bags! But that's a small percentage of the population. This is where many Asian businesses have missed out. The cream is in the 65 million other people who don't have a chance to fly, who don't have credit cards or insurance. I always saw the masses. I always felt easier with the masses, to be honest, because I love people. So I know what people want. I enjoy bringing in services. It's a great feeling."

Tony has not only created an airline that allows everyone to fly, he has created an airline anyone can come and work for, without any aviation experience. His empowerment of over 17,000 staff with no unions, and the ability to "take someone with no experience and put them into a very senior role" is what makes the airline a standout success in Asia. Tony derives the greatest satisfaction from having helped build careers and believing in people when others didn't. The unrelenting determination that Tony displays, and inspires in his staff, should allow AirAsia to surmount most of the hurdles in the evolving aviation industry. He embodies a brand X-factor that has been replicated by few other airlines in the world.

6X Analysis

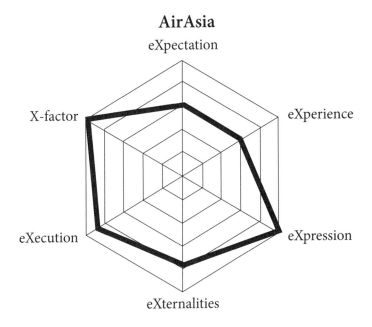

AirAsia
eXpectation

X-factor

eXperience

eXecution

eXpression

eXternalities

Personified by Tony Fernandes, the AirAsia brand inspires bold actions by its staff. Since he has empowered his team to use their creativity in solving problems and to exercise their own judgment in making decisions, the brand **eXpression** within AirAsia is astounding. Everyone can chart their own career and move around the organization with ease. This freedom to express then comes across to the passengers aboard AirAsia flights, who can get a wholehearted response with ease from the flight attendants and social media channels alike. Dedicated brand **eXecution** at AirAsia is what makes the airline tick—from its focus on quick turnarounds for aircraft, to how employees like Yap Mun Ching were given full responsibility to lead projects end-to-end. Its execution of core brand values keeps AirAsia in a leadership position among low-cost airlines globally.

4: TURKISH AIRLINES: DELIGHTFULLY DIFFERENT

By 2012, Turkish Airlines had grown so much that it flew to more countries than any other airline in the world. Until recently, it had leveraged its low-cost base—on a par with the likes of Ryanair and easyJet—to offer competitive fares. The low fares filled the seats. But there was a problem: Not many people knew about Turkish Airlines outside its core markets. According to public surveys conducted in 2011, brand recall for the airline was around 34 percent—not ideal for a global brand trying to punch above its weight.

To drive global awareness, the airline decided they would need to enlist the services of a celebrity who had global recognition. In 2009 they launched a global marketing campaign entitled "Feel Like a Star," featuring Hollywood actor Kevin Costner. While the campaign drove awareness in key markets, the feedback they received was that Kevin Costner's persona didn't align well with the young and fresh brand Turkish Airlines was trying to create.

Learning quickly, the team then trained their focus on sports marketing. Turkish Airlines sponsored football clubs Manchester United and FC Barcelona. That drove instant awareness in Europe,

Asia, and Africa, where the clubs are very popular. To gain a foothold in the United States and Japan, they started supporting basketball star Kobe Bryant. But the airline knew that to drive true engagement, they had to go beyond putting their name on jerseys or painting airplanes.

There was also the constraint that Turkish Airlines did not have the agreement to feature all players of the teams in a singe advertisement. That's when the interactive and digital team stepped in. Turkish Airlines realized that the individual players in the teams they sponsored often have a greater brand resonance than the club itself. Case in point: Lionel Messi, who is incredibly popular anywhere soccer is played or watched. Messi, an Argentinean, had been playing football since he was two and had become one of the most popular stars of the game owing to being the top scorer in the Champions League for three years.

Across the Atlantic, Kobe Bryant was the youngest athlete ever to play in the NBA, and was named slam-dunk champion. He had two Olympic gold medals to his name and led his team, the LA Lakers, to the NBA Championship five times. Adding Kobe to the mix would certainly up the chances of creating a potential global hit of an advertisement. The trick would be to combine that star power with a memorable, well-executed campaign.

The Turkish Airlines interactive team partnered with their agency, CP&B in London, to think hard about how to launch a video advertisement that had the potential to go viral online. In the immediate aftermath of Korean pop star Psy's global hit with his "Gangnam Style" video, everyone was trying to figure out the formula.

The underlying purpose of the video was to showcase Turkish Airlines' product, specifically the business class cabin and the food. To increase the appeal, a cute young kid was chosen to be the protagonist. A storyline was developed in which Messi and Kobe compete for the kid's attention by performing ball tricks in their respective sports. From ball tricks the competition escalates to card tricks, then balloon animals of increasingly improbable complexity. In the end, a flight attendant, who wins the kid over with the offer of ice cream, foils the efforts of both stars. The stage was set: two sports megastars, ball tricks, a cute kid, and ice cream—all in a single video!

The interactive team did not want to leave any stone unturned in driving the maximum coverage for the video. Turkish Airlines became one of the first airlines in the world to create and execute a professional seeding plan to ensure a video spreads far and wide. Key YouTube influencers and bloggers in identified markets were engaged ahead of time to post the video link on their profiles once it was released. Teasers were released to drum up anticipation before the official video launch, just like a Hollywood movie trailer. Advertising dollars were committed to promoting the video in key target markets as well.

On December 6, 2012, the day the video went live on YouTube, all those well-planned actions were set in motion. Each action triggered another, and the marketing plan worked like dominos. On the second day after launch, the video was covered by major news outlets like the Los Angeles Times and Fox News. By the third day, #kobevsmessi became a trending topic on social media, allowing even more people to discover the video. On the fourth day, the video hit 20 million views on YouTube—a feat that Gangnam style took 30 days to accomplish. Turkish Airlines had created the fastest spreading video in history.

Within a week of launch, the video had been viewed 35 million times in more than 220 countries. Ultimately, it reached more than 111 million views, more than any other online video in history.

Turkish Airlines' success in driving global awareness of its product via an online video was not a fluke, but a carefully planned and executed effort unlike any before it in aviation marketing.

It was, in fact, a concerted strategy that was being pushed hand-in-hand with Turkish's stellar network expansion, in order to raise the brand's global profile.

After all, Turkish Airlines is perfectly situated on the globe to be an international airline with a huge network. Istanbul has a unique geographical situation. If you fly three hours to the North, and West, and South, and East, you can connect almost 100 countries with each other.

As Chief Marketing Officer Ahmet Olmustur told us "Well, our brand value—I think we started from around $5 million, almost 10 years ago. Now it is $2.2 billion. Five years ago, only 38 percent of people in the world knew about Turkish Airlines. Today, that number is around 65 percent."

While the airline's network growth was phenomenal, what was needed simultaneously was a marketing push that would secure its fortunes as one of the most recognizable airlines in the world. Kobe versus Messi delivered precisely that.

The Second Phase Begins

It has been a long journey this past decade. Turkish Airlines' immense network is something the airline is rightly proud of. But you can sense that the journey has only just begun in earnest. Brand recognition, appreciation, network expansion are all in the bag. Turkish Airlines is now well known in over 100 countries. Smart network choices and aggressive marketing have brought them to an interesting stage of growth.

Ahmet says, "We did lots of things in the last 12 years. But now we feel like there is room to improve on the quality of our products. So, we're focusing our studies to how can we move forward in terms of increasing customer appreciation. Just because of that, earlier in 2016, we just created a new department that is responsible for the Customer Experience Management. We carried about sixty million passengers in the last year —we believe that we can increase the loyalty of our customer passengers also by increasing customer appreciation. The clincher comes as Ahmet adds, "But now we're just focusing on the quality of product." And what a remarkable product it is.

A Well-Choreographed In-Flight Meal Performance

The last thing you would expect on an airplane is a candle. But about 45 minutes after the takeoff of my Turkish Airlines flight from Toronto to Istanbul, the flight attendants in the Business Class cabin rolled out a trolley topped with beautiful, flickering candles. There were no open flames, but electric lamps smartly dressed with translucent origami paper. One of these was placed on my table just before the meals were served. Turkish Airlines' candlelit dinner in the air is one of the things that makes the experience of flying on the airline delightfully different for its passengers.

Even before the candles were rolled out, I was already quite impressed by the in-flight chef, dressed in white overalls, a tie, and a distinctive toque. It is the chef, rather than a flight attendant, who serves the meals in business class. After they have graduated from culinary school, Turkish Airlines gives their chefs three months of additional training to get them up to speed on preparing and serving food on their aircraft as well as in the airline's lounge.

On my flight, the chef started by setting my dinner table with salt and pepper shakers, which had tops that looked like Ottoman hats. He then served me green tea in a Chinese earthen pot. Pumpkin soup was next, poured into a ceramic bowl with a golden inner lining. Finally came the dessert, served on a Turkish-lattice steel rack. The chef placed the accompanying teapot on a traditional Turkish boiler to keep it warm.

The food lived up to its captivating presentation. The soup was fresh, the Turkish mezze appetizing, and the main course of lamb shish kebab was marinated in Turkish spices that brought me to

Istanbul long before my plane touched down. Of course, having an on-board chef serve me all these delicacies made them all the more impressive.

To my surprise and delight, after the flight attendants cleared the dinner away, they left the candles on the seats, which created a lovely ambience when the cabin lights were dimmed.

One of the fundamental tenets of branding is that even the most innovative and far-reaching marketing campaign will not succeed if it is not backed up by a strong product. The dining experience on Turkish Airlines, the pleasures of which linger long after the flight, is just one example of the excellence of the airline's product offering. Chief Commercial Officer Akif Konar said, "It's not only eating something or drinking something. We see the catering as part of the enjoyment on board."

Food being a critical part of the Turkish Airlines brand, a great deal of thought and planning went into its superior meal preparation and delivery.

To design its meal service, Turkish Airlines created a joint venture with Austria's Do&Co in 2007. Do&Co was already famous for serving delicacies to VIPs at Formula One races and at UEFA football championships. The mission of the new company, Turkish Do&Co, was to create a wow factor in onboard meals and surprise the passengers.

The joint venture focused on excelling at three key elements for the meal service: the quality of the food, its presentation, and the presenter. This focus ensures that the meals consistently taste fresh and delicious, and they are served in a unique fashion by chefs who pay attention to detail. For example, in order to preserve its taste, the food is never frozen—a rare practice in the airline industry.

When the new meal program was launched in 2010, the chefs only served business class passengers on long-haul flights. But the service has proven popular, winning many travel industry awards, so the airline has gradually introduced chefs into business class on medium-haul flights as well. While the onboard chefs only serve the business class passengers, they maintain the high quality of the meals served in all cabins. Elements of surprise are strewn throughout the flight, too. The success of the on-board meal service is due not only to all the choices the airline has made about the food and its delivery, but also the choices they've made about other aspects of the flight. One choice in particular was about what service not to include. Few may notice, but the airline does not have onboard shopping. There are no carts with branded perfumes and cosmetics being rolled out halfway through a flight. As Temel Kotil, Turkish Airlines' CEO, explained, "We don't want to dilute the culinary experience. That is our focus and we want people to remember only that."

Creating the Most Viral YouTube Ad in History—Twice

Just as the smartest marketing strategy in the world will not succeed without a strong product to back it up, the inverse is true as well. Customers will not flock to a great product if they don't know it exists.

Turkish Airlines has been investing heavily in its onboard experience and its lounge for nearly 10 years. For about that same period, the airline has been working to expand its global footprint. But for the first five of those years, their global brand recognition was lagging behind the excellence of their product. About five years ago, however, the airline dramatically upped its marketing game, with spectacular results.

In fact, despite their global campaigns and advertisements, Turkish Airlines has done exceedingly well in key local markets as well. In Japan, for instance, Turkish Airlines sensed an opportunity to gain popularity among the Japanese travelers who preferred to travel to off-beat destinations. Given the airline's vast network, this was, on paper, a match made in heaven. But still, the match needed to be made.

Continuing their success with sports marketing, the airline began by sponsoring the national basketball league. The marketing team came up with the concept of Basukettoke, a unique dance with three basic moves, symbolizing power, courage, and victory. To popularize this dance during basketball games, Turkish Airlines created a micro-website that hosted guidance videos on how to do the Basukettoke. Then Japanese basketball fans were encouraged to post their own videos of themselves doing the dance. The videos would be entered into a competition for the best moves, and prizes would be given to the best dancers, called the Basukettoke Masters.

Japanese fans loved Basukettoke and the dance spread rapidly among them. Hundreds of fans uploaded their own videos and eleven won Turkish Airlines–sponsored prizes. Ultimately, the campaign created 32 million impressions online. More importantly, 32,000 basketball fans at the Ariake Coliseum performed the Basukettoke energetically during the league finals, and they were broadcast on television and cable channels across Japan. Turkish Airlines had become a phenomenon in Japan.

Now, let's get back to the global arena.

After the runaway success of the first Messi–Kobe video, the challenge before the team was to do even better for the next one. No small task, but the team set themselves a target of 150 million views for the second video.

Typically for digital videos, companies think about the content strategy first and distribution second. Turkish Airlines' agency, CP&B, led the effort by thinking first about channels the video would be distributed on and how they would be optimized, before they began developing the actual content of the video.

As in the earlier Kobe–Messi video, YouTube was the key focus channel, and the new video would be spread with a mix of advertisements and influencer shout-outs, which would drive social sharing. But on this go-round, brand awareness would be heightened by optimizing the advertisements for clicks that would bring viewers to Turkish Airlines' website, where they could learn more about all the destinations around the world that the airline services. To drive further awareness, the team would reach out to the press in a systematic manner at specific times before and after launch of the video. They also established metrics for each distribution channel, from comments and watch-rate percentage on YouTube, to conversions and cost-per-acquisition for clicks leading to the website.

In the week leading up the video, the team would repeat the successful strategy of releasing a teaser to incite curiosity and anticipation. After the release of the video, Turkish Airlines' 20,000 employees would become brand ambassadors. They would be given access to a dedicated Facebook tab that was normally used to share company news, only now the airline's staff would be using it to share the video with their friends.

With the distribution plan in place, the team focused on content. This time they wanted to drive awareness of the fact that Turkish Airlines flew to more countries than any other airline in the world. Having had over-the-top success with Kobe Bryant and Lionel Messi, they went with the duo again. They decided to see if they could up the ante on the friendly competition between the stars as well, as that had resonated so strongly in the first video. Then the question was what to do with all those ingredients.

This was 2013, and the Oxford English Dictionary had named "selfie" the word of the year. Since the selfie craze had been catalyzed by travelers around the world, the agency and the airline decided to leverage the phenomenon—no airline had owned the concept till then. "Kobe v. Messi: the Selfie Shootout" was born, with each star trying to out-do the other by taking selfies in the coolest spots around the world.

Messi kicked things off with a selfie using the Kremlin as a backdrop. Kobe one-upped him by posing on the Great Wall of China. Messi posed underwater near a reef in the Maldives, and Kobe came back by posing with a great white shark in the waters off Cape Town. Messi posed on the summit of Mount Kilimanjaro, but then Kobe came floating along above Messi's head in a hang glider. In the climactic scene, Messi posed in front of the Hagia Sophia in Turkish Airlines' home, Istanbul. Not to be outdone, Kobe photo-bombed him just as he was snapping the picture.

Now it was time to see if the distribution strategy combined with the content could create magic for the airline a second time. When the video went live, it did well, though the initial take up was not as fast as the original video. But it soon picked up speed. The strategy of seeding the video with key YouTube influencers helped a lot with growth in views and shares. The audience enjoyed the suspense element of the video, where they were always wondering how and where the stars would try to top each other. They very much liked the ending, in which the two run off in opposite directions on the streets of Istanbul and the fight continues. People were left wanting more. This resulted in the average play duration being longer the actual one-minute duration of the video. In other words, people were rewinding and watching certain parts again.

Ultimately, the video reached 142 million views within a month and had 1.2 million social shares. It was selected as the YouTube Advertisement of the Decade and there were over two thousand press features around the world.

Turkish Airlines had more up their sleeve. They soon followed up the video with a Turkish Airlines selfie app, where anyone could submit and upload selfies to win a prize, tickets to any Turkish Airlines destinations. Regular contests were held over the next year to encourage further participation. They set up selfie stands in various cities as well. This gave the public some skin in the game and took brand participation to new heights. Thanks to a partnership with TripAdvisor, the application was downloaded over 30,000 times. Turkish Airlines was the first major airline to use YouTube as a focus platform for its global marketing efforts. Video views came from nearly every country the airline flies to. And by the time the second video became a hit, top-of-mind awareness had risen from 34 percent to more than 60 percent—a major achievement for the airline.

One of the World's Best Lounges

In step with their continued marketing coups, Turkish has not paused its relentless push to create some of the most memorable travel experiences for passengers. Their lounge stands testimony to their belief that the experience must live up to the perception even on the ground, not just in-flight.

Managed by Turkish Do&Co, Lounge Istanbul is perhaps one of the best in the world, and serves great meals to Turkish Airlines' business class passengers and those with a Star Alliance Gold status. The excellent culinary experience extends to the ground as well. The airline's chefs also serve meals to premium passengers who visit the airline's lounge in Istanbul.

The lounge has three "Live Food" sections, one for Turkish cuisine, one for world cuisine, and one for seasonal food. All of the Live stations are manned by Turkish Do&Co chefs, who rotate between serving passengers in the lounge and in the air. At the Turkish station you will find unique dishes like Turkish pide, freshly baked in a brick oven, while Italian pasta and other global delicacies are available at the World station. Visitors to the lounge can even find a popcorn station and, of course, a Turkish Delight station.

But the virtues of the lounge extend beyond food. At 6,000 square meters, Lounge Istanbul is larger than some airports. The lounge has an iconic design. As you enter, a pool table and a library welcome you. There are beautifully lit private storage lockers—they are transparent and look like jewel boxes. Once you've left your bags in a locker, you can make yourself comfortable in a variety of sections, including a shower and sleeping pods if you have a long layover.

For such a large space, it has been well designed for travelers with a variety of interests. On one visit, you could be playing a round of virtual golf, or a game of pool, or even racing model cars on a custom track. On another, you might immerse yourself in Ottoman history in the exclusive library or you might listen to Frank Sinatra in the theatre.

The lounge offers so many different experiences that you are bound to discover something new if you take a walk around. Only on my seventh visit did I realize that in addition to the massage beds, there's a roving massage therapist in case you want a shoulder massage! Lounge Istanbul is a destination in itself, and the first major brand touch point for travelers departing from Istanbul. It provides a refreshing solace for transit passengers as well.

Destination Marketing

While the airline broke one record after another in its efforts to drive global awareness, it also stepped up efforts in important individual markets to connect with the locals at a deeper level. This was a different kind of challenge. Turkish Airlines needed to tailor their approach to the specific temperaments of some of their key national markets.

When Turkish Airlines decided to launch flights from Istanbul to San Francisco in 2014, its seventh destination in the United States, they wasted no time in creating a marketing campaign that would drive awareness of the new route. This would be especially important because San Francisco is one of the most competitive long-haul markets in the world.

In the recent years, the likes of Emirates and Etihad have launched new flights to the city. Though the Turkish Airlines hub at Istanbul is technically in Europe, it is close enough to the Gulf hubs that the competition for passengers with these Middle Eastern airlines is intense.

For launching the Turkish Airlines Istanbul–San Francisco route, the airline went with a holistic marketing approach. Their efforts were driven by four key initiatives.

The Livery

Turkish Airlines commissioned a Boeing 777-300ER to sport an exclusive livery signifying the link between Istanbul and San Francisco. Bright, stylized paintings showcased iconic locations in Istanbul on one side of the plane and iconic San Francisco paintings on the other. This helped generate interest in the route among the close-knit and vocal community of aviation geeks and plane spotters, which in turn was amplified on social media. Turkish Airlines' official presence on social channels helped to drive the reach even further.

Importantly, the 777-300ER was not limited to flying only the Istanbul-to-San Francisco route, so anyone at any airport in the world who sees this aircraft will be able to draw the link between Istanbul and San Francisco.

Creative Content Marketing

Although Turkish Airlines carries a lot of connecting traffic, it also has the great advantage of having a distinguished cultural capital like Istanbul as its hub. To promote Istanbul as a cultural destination, Turkish Airlines smartly partnered with viral content website BuzzFeed to co-create listicles that highlighted the city and its connections with San Francisco. For example, the post "15 Reasons San Francisco and Istanbul are Long-Lost Sister Cities" featured pairs of complementary photos linking the two cities. BuzzFeed's substantial reach and popularity, especially in the United States, helped bring a level of awareness to the route that would have been unlikely from conventional advertising.

The business half of the second marketing initiative entailed letting the world know that Istanbul was a new epicenter of the tech startup world, "the Silicon Valley of Eurasia." In the spring of 2016, in collaboration with the Istanbul-based creative agency Efrabrika, Turkish Airlines created a humorous video called "Startup Class." The video promotes tech-related travel from the San Francisco Bay Area to Istanbul by poking fun at the foibles and pretensions of tech people. The punchline: One guy's app is "like Instagram, but for cat photos," while the other's is a dating app for drones called "Dromance." As of the writing of this chapter, the video has surpassed 1.3 million views.

Global Binoculars

Collaborating again with Efrabrika, Turkish Airlines custom-made a modern version of the tourist binoculars one finds along beautiful city coastlines or on the observation decks of skyscrapers. Except rather than magnifying the view, these binoculars show tourists beautiful 360-degree photographs and videos of all the destinations around the world that Turkish Airlines flies to. The binoculars, made from aircraft aluminum, were labeled with the airline's slogan, "Widen Your World," and installed at key tourist points around San Francisco. The binoculars gave San Francisco locals and tourists another opportunity to associate the city with the airline and all the other places in the world to which it could deliver them. More than six thousand people tried the binoculars in just four days.

The San Francisco route launch, above all, signifies the sharp marketing mind that Turkish has developed over the years. Not only can it execute the biggest advertising blockbusters on the internet, its marketing machine is equally capable of assessing key markets and destinations and tailoring initiatives to their needs. From Kobe–Messi's grand scale to Japan's impressively localized execution, to San Francisco's holistic initiatives, Turkish Airlines proves that it's not just money that makes marketing. Strategy is, reassuringly, still king.

20,000 young CEOs

We have discussed Turkish Airlines' considerable strengths in the areas of product and marketing. Now it is time to turn our attention to the third crucial element that comprises brand: company culture. Not that these three elements are fully separable, as you will see.

In February, Turkish Airlines' Interactive Marketing Communication Manager Neset Dereli was at the Ploshchad Revolyutsii Metro station in Moscow, where he spotted a statue of a dog whose nose was worn away. He discovered that this was because of the legend that if you rub the nose of the dog, you will be showered with good luck. Instead of just sharing his encounter with the lucky dog nose with his friends on Facebook or Whatsapp, he submitted it as a travel tip to the Turkish Airlines "Widen Your World" blog.

The blog is entirely crewsourced—i.e., all entries are written by Turkish Airlines staff. While they are not the only airline with an engaging blog, most of the others contain articles about destinations and travel written by a syndicate of writers or reprinted from the in-flight magazine. No one has been assigned to write for Turkish Airlines' blog—contributions are voluntary.

The content strategy for the blog entails prioritizing the top destinations for the airline, and then asking the staff to volunteer to submit content on those destinations. They may submit as many entries as they want. Some are planned, others impromptu. You may wonder, why employees? The answer: because airline employees—crew and non-crew alike—are some of the most widely traveled individuals, and have lots of travel stories to share.

The blog bears some similarity to TripAdvisor, only created by

Turkish Airlines' employees for their passengers. The many cities covered include Antalya, Addis Ababa, Stockholm, Baku, New Delhi, and Sao Paolo. You can read brief travel anecdotes, get travel tips, look at maps, and of course, meet the more than 50 authors who've contributed to the blog so far. So the blog is a marketing tool that also enhances company culture by empowering employees and giving them public recognition for their travel observations and insights. But the synergy between marketing and culture goes deeper than that.

The secret sauce behind Turkish Airlines' spectacular marketing efforts in the last few years is that most of the company's managers and even its executives are in their early-to-mid thirties. The new SVP of marketing is a 35 year old lady. The CIO is less than 35, and the chief marketing officer is only 34 years of age. In fact, there is hardly anyone older than Temel Kotil, the CEO, who is 56. And that is intentional.

Temel bey, as he is known affectionately within the airline, is an aeronautics professor, and his propensity for hiring people in their 20s and 30s arises out of his instincts as a teacher. He believes that like the students of his teaching days, his young employees have as much to teach him as vice versa. Especially relevant to the airline business, they are tuned in to the latest technological developments, are well versed in English and often other European languages, and have a lot more international exposure than the older generation.

The younger managers, when given larger responsibilities, also tend to work harder. Hiring younger people makes hard work part of the DNA of the airline. As Temel bey has said, "I have 20,000 CEOs helping me do my job better." He believes in putting his full faith in the young managers and empowering them, at the risk of initial failures. "Perhaps in the first six months," he told us, "they will fail often. But they will work here about 30 years. So they can make up that loss very easily."

As in other industries, the younger generation of executives and managers have different expectations. They not only want empowerment, they also want recognition and access to the top. To enable this, Temel bey has emailed his personal mobile number to all 9,000 cabin crew as well as all senior managers across divisions. When there's a serious enough issue, they can get directly in touch with him and seek immediate resolution.

In contrast to Turkish Airlines' approach, most other airlines' upper ranks are filled with industry veterans. The advantage is their wealth of experience, but the potential disadvantage is less fresh thinking and over-attachment to the old way of doing things.

Especially in the marketing division, the advantage of having young people in decision-making positions is evident, as they've leveraged trends like the selfie and capitalized on platforms like YouTube to build a global brand that has seen awareness increase multifold in the past decade.

What Does the Future Hold?

Turkish Airlines is flying to 241 international destinations and has another 60 coming in the next few years. It has a very strong on-board product and thanks to its innovative marketing, global awareness of the brand has grown dramatically in recent years. But the externalities the airline now faces will almost certainly be the biggest challenge in the airline's next chapter. Conflicts in the region have spilled over in recent times, resulting in terrorist attacks within Turkey. As Brett Snyder of the popular aviation blog CrankyFlier bluntly put it, "If you had to pick one airline in the world that you'd hate to be running right now, Turkish would be at the top of the list."

But Temel bey looks at it differently. He believes that, "Terrorism is not against one country, it is against the world. Although I am not an expert on terrorism, a way to fight this is to promote traveling. There is no physical danger to come to Istanbul, I can go any place I want in the middle of the night in Istanbul. It is the same for Athens,

Munich, Atlanta. I am telling everyone not to be hesitant to travel, to the governments not to issue warning, not to scare people to travel. The aim of terrorist attacks is to spread fear, if nobody fears, then the terror will perish by its nature. The more people travel, the less terror there will be." Despite Temel bey's hopeful outlook, challenges remain. The airline needs to recognize the threats security issues cause to the brand and address them in meaningful ways.

Turkish Airlines also has to contend with the fact that Istanbul Ataturk is now operating at capacity, while the airline continues to grow. Economy-class passengers without access to the spacious lounge have to put up with a certain amount of congestion during peak travel periods until the new Istanbul airport—slated to be seven times larger than Ataturk—is up and running in 2018. In the meantime Turkish Airlines, has alleviated their passengers' pain by creating more wi-fi hotspots in the airport. We recommend they also work with the airport authorities to add more electrical outlets, since all the wi-fi in the world will not help you if your phone, laptop, or tablet is dead.

Apart from facing down geopolitical instability and minimizing customer inconvenience as they await a more spacious and modern airport, the airline's current focus is on taking what is already an outstanding customer experience and standardizing it. They have done very well in creating a high level in cabin service. Though, because of their exponential growth in the past decade, they need to catch up by creating consistent standards of excellence across all touch points, especially on the ground. At the moment, they're operating on an evolving customer life cycle model of 66 touch points to ensure that the enjoyable customer experience in the air is replicated on the ground both before and after the flight. For example, the airline has recently launched a complimentary chauffer service for its business-class passengers to extend the experience beyond the flight.

Turkish Airlines has shown itself to be agile, smart, and capable of delivering a superior product as it has expanded into a competitive global market. We will be watching with great curiosity to see how they handle the formidable challenges coming their way.

6X Analysis

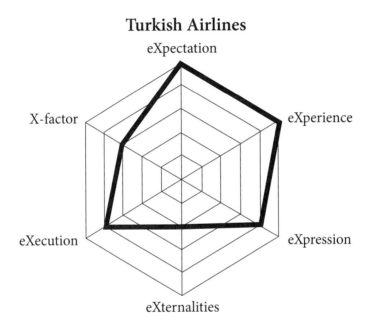

Without a doubt, Turkish Airlines' superlative brand elements are **eXperience** and **eXpectation**, or, to put it in the terms we've been using throughout the chapter, the product and the marketing. They are also quite strong on **eXpression**.

The airline does so well on the **eXperience** scorecard because they have taken a positive characteristic for which Turkey as a whole is known—hospitality—and made that a signature feature of the experience both in the air and in the lounge, where well-trained chefs stylishly serve beautifully prepared meals. They are a premium airline that goes head-to-head with fancy competitors like Emirates, not by emulating them, but by differentiating themselves.

Thanks to Kobe Bryant, Lionel Messi, thousands of Japanese basketball fans, Silicon Valley tech entrepreneurs, and the brilliant marketing team that connected them and their admirers to the Turkish Airlines brand, the airline does very well in the **eXpectation** category. Creative global marketing of their extensive footprint has let customers know they can pretty much pick any country in the world out of a hat and be confident that Turkish Airlines will fly there.

Finally, in the **eXpression** category, the airline gives their staff prominent exposure through the "Widen Your World" website. And Temel bey communicates his confidence in the abilities of his young management team by letting them know that mistakes are to be expected as they climb the steep learning curve of the airline industry during their first months on the job.

Southwest

Herb Kelleher and his quotes adorn many walls at Southwest's headquarters

Southwest staff see the new livery with the heart for the first time

The state of the art social listening center at Southwest allows the airline to keep a pulse of digital channels and respond in real-time

The refreshed boarding process at Southwest reduces the anxiety that came with first-come-first-served seating

Trans**fare**ncy℠
Low fares. Nothing to hide.

	1st Checked Bag	2nd Checked Bag	Flight Change Fee	Other Select Fees	Feels Like
Southwest	$0	$0	$0	$0	Winning!
American	$25	$35	$200	$205	Yikes.
United	$25	$35	$200	$250	Ooof.
Spirit	$30	$40	$110	$262	We lost track.
Delta	$25	$35	$200	$200	Whaaat?!
Virgin	$25	$25	$100	$140	Arrgh.
JetBlue	$20	$35	$70	$125	Really.

#FeesDontFly

Southwest⬦

Transfarency campaign takes a dig at other airlines charging for peripheries that Southwest never did

Finnair

Finnair's design collaboration with Marimekko
comes to life on its aircraft and crockery

The northern lights effect on display in Finnair's Airbus A350 aircraft

The Ultima Thule glass, designed by the legendary Tapio Wirkkala

AirAsia

From dispatch boy to Airbus 320 Pilot...

Kugan Tangiisuran gets recognized on Facebook
for rising from dispatch boy to pilot at AirAsia

Tony Fernandes @tonyfernandes 21 hrs
I as your group ceo will be there through these hard times. We will go
through this terrible ordeal together ... tmi.me/1eVa7A

   683   386

Tony Fernandes @tonyfernandes 21 hrs
To all my staff Airasia all stars be strong,
continue to be the best. Pray hard. Continue
to do your best for all our guests. See u all
soon

   2.2K   1K

Tony Fernandes tweets emphatically to AirAsia staff
after the crash of one of its aircrafts in December 2014

Sir Richard Branson dresses up as an AirAsia flight attendant
and serves Tony Fernandes in-flight, after losing a bet

Turkish Airlines

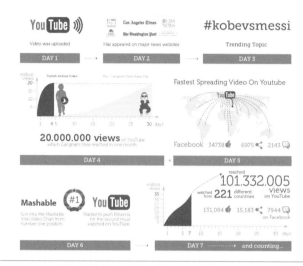

How Kobe vs Messi became the most
watched advertisement on YouTube

Origami candles being rolled out
on Turkish Airlines Business Class

The focus on food continues at the Lounge
in Istanbul with freshly baked pide

The lounge has a huge library and a pool table
to welcome weary travelers

kulula

Flying 101 – kulula's viral hit

The tounge-in-cheek kulula advertisement

kulula's culture wall in the crew briefing room

Singapore Airlines

Two Singapore Airlines print advertisements that
featured the Singapore Girl in the early days of the airline

A recent Singapore Airlines advertisement
continues the focus on the Singapore Girl

Luca Iaconi-Stewart created a highly detailed aircraft model for
Singapore Airlines made entirely of recycled manila folders

Air New Zealand

The "Nothing to Hide" advertisement where staff appeared in body paint, which started it all for Air New Zealand

I try out Air New Zealand's Skycouch™ on board the Dreamliner 787

Rico, Air New Zealand's furry mascot on the Skycouch™
with David Hasselhoff

A passenger uses the in-flight chat system to notify me that
the Kiwi Prime Minister is seated right behind me!

5: KULULA.COM: THE WORLD'S FUNNIEST AIRLINE

"The Hardest Part of Your Trip"

In my years of working with airlines and analyzing what makes an airline brand successful, one thing that has become clear to me is that there is no universal formula for success. What works in one market may not work in another. Recall that Joyce Lai, who was head of marketing in the early days of AirAsia, said they did not emphasize the *fun* aspects of the brand back then because, as she put it, "Can you imagine, low cost, fun, funky? It would be like, my gosh, is this an airline, or what?" There are, on the one hand, important similarities between AirAsia and kulula.com. They both started in 2001 as the first low-cost carriers on their respective continents, Asia and Africa. Both were small and feisty and punching above their weight. But on the other hand, while AirAsia downplayed *fun and funky* in the early days, kulula made it a core component of their brand identity from the start. So the two airlines were trying to achieve similar goals, and each developed its brand identity based on a deep understanding of who their customers were and what would make them keep coming back.

Michael O'Leary, CEO of the Irish low-cost carrier RyanAir, has famously said, "What's brand? Brand is nothing. Price is the product." kulula's management begs to differ. Even in the first several years of the domestic South African airline's existence, when it was the only low-cost carrier in all of Africa, kulula was working hard and working smart to create an identity that went well beyond beating its competitors on fares. As Brian Kitchin, Executive Manager of Sales, said, "The challenge wasn't really price at the beginning. The challenge was to get people to put their credit card into an online system that was rather a new concept with regards to shopping in South Africa ." kulula rose to the challenge in a lot of ways, but if there's one element of the airline's personality that passengers think of first, it's probably their humor. Across all touchpoints, even ones you wouldn't expect, kulula uses humor to separate itself. Humor alone doesn't build trust, of course. You've got to be safe and reliable; you've got to offer not just low prices but also good value; and particularly for a customer base that was unfamiliar with all aspects of flying in those early days—from booking a ticket, to navigating an airport, to knowing how to put on an oxygen mask, to claiming your baggage—you've got to be easy to use. kulula has always delivered on all those things, and the vehicle of delivery has consistently been humor. It is woven in most interactions of the airline with the passengers, on board the flights, and beyond.

As a way of tracking the meaning and effect of kulula's humorous brand identity, let's imagine a novice flyer's experience of the brand from the first touchpoint to the last. Along the way, we'll meet some of the kulula staff who create and maintain the brand, and we'll examine their strategies for becoming what they are now— one of the dominant African low-cost airlines, carrying millions of customers each year.

Starting with the first touchpoint: kulula's ads are funny. In the early days, in a country where until recently only a few could afford to fly, kulula put up billboards with photographs of ordinary South Africans dressed in "super fan" outfits, with bright kulula-green capes and propeller-beanies. One of the most viewed of kulula's many TV/video ads is a 20-second spot that shows a woman in a small hotel room trying to close her overstuffed, inexpensive-looking yellow suitcase. She sits on it, she kneels on it, she jumps on it, she falls on it, she slams it into a wall. She attacks it, shall we say, suggestively. Finally, she gets it closed, sighs with relief, and starts walking away, but the hem of her long skirt turns out to have been caught inside, and she falls down—a beautifully executed classic slapstick pratfall. This is clearly not an ad targeted to business travelers and seasoned vacationers. This everywoman represents people new to the rigors of air travel, or still learning the ropes. The video's tagline is "The hardest part of your trip," followed by the tagline, "Keeping it easy." It's no coincidence that the word "kulula" traces its origin to the Zulu word meaning "easy".

If you are a new or relatively inexperienced flyer, you look at this ad, which hooks you in with laughter, and maybe you think, "Okay, I don't really know much about air travel, but if that goofball can do it, so can I. After all, I haven't visited my mother in months." So you go to the website, maybe your first time on an airline's website, and you are relieved to find a page called "kulula 101." It's got infographics, some highly informative reading material, and some fun instructional videos. Maybe, as Brian Kitchin suggested, you're skeptical about feeding your credit card number into an airline's website. So you click on the infographic entitled "Where does your money go?" It's a pie chart that tells you 24 percent of the price of your ticket goes to fuel, 18 percent to aircraft and maintenance costs, 10 percent to staff, and so on. And then you go to the instructional videos, narrated by someone called the "How to Fly Guy." He explains that instead of standing in a long line at the airport to check in, you can save time and check in with your mobile phone. As Mike Ilsley, Executive Manager of IT, Contact Centre and CIO, told us, a lot of South Africa's population, particularly outside of the big cities, does not have easy access to reliable broadband internet connections. So the mobile phone piece is really going to appeal to that crucial demographic. If you're new to booking online, there's a video about how to do that. And if you're like the woman in the ad who gets her skirt caught in her suitcase, there's even an instructional video about packing your bag.

"Those Seatbelts Fastened Tight around Those Gorgeous Hips"

So you've bought your ticket, you've packed your bag, you arrive at the airport, and then you see something very unexpected coming towards you. It seems to be... a bathtub... on wheels... with a kulula-green rubber duck floating on its bubbly waters. And there's someone inside the bathtub, someone you recognize. Who is it? It's South African comedian Siv Ngesi. He's got a phone in his hand. And he's doing online check-in on that phone. From his bathtub!

Yes, in November 2014, just in time for the holidays, kulula launched a fun stunt for those passengers who may not have found their way to the How to Fly Guy's instructional online check-in video: celebrities in remote-controlled bathtubs-on-wheels—or beds-on-wheels—rolling around the airport, showing you how to check in for your flight online and save yourself from standing in the long holiday lines at the airport.

You've made it through check-in and security, and you've managed to dodge all the rolling bathtubs and beds coming at you down the airport corridors. Now you're sitting in a chair at your gate with your overstuffed carry-on bag at your side. If you're a first-time flyer, maybe you're a little nervous, so you take a peek out the window at your plane. And a big grin spreads across your face. The plane is the same color as the rubber duck in the bathtub, bright green. And it's got all kinds of white lettering on it. In the biggest letters of all, across the starboard side of the fuselage, is the phrase "Flying 101." In smaller lettering, just below that, are the words "front door," with an arrow pointing toward, you guessed it, the front door of the plane. Forward of the door is "co-captain," with an arrow pointing to the co-captain's window. Below that is "nose cone." There's also "fuel tank," "black box," "landing gear," "seats," "loo," "kulula fans" (arrows pointing toward passenger windows), and a dozen or so other labels. This aircraft went so viral on the internet, that even before Facebook was popular, photos of the aircraft attached would be circulated over emails and I would get one of those every couple of weeks from someone in the industry!

This plane, eponymously known as "Flying 101," was the brain-child of Cherese Wansink, head of kulula's in-house design team. In 2010, when she came up with the idea, she was just a junior designer. Management loved it right away. This tells you something about kulula's corporate structure and ethos. Since kulula often runs topical advertisements that touch on current events, it's been very handy for them to have an in-house team as well as an external agency ensuring quick turnarounds so the ads are out in the public while the subject is still fresh. So in April of 2012, when South African's President Jacob Zuma married his fourth wife, kulula ran a promotion titled "Fourth Wife Flies Free." They even tagged President Zuma on their Facebook page. They were joking, but they were not kidding: the text of the ad says, "Inspired by regular VIP travelers with sizeable spousal entourages, the offer is open to all fourth wives when the family travels together on the Jo'burg to Cape Town route." And in 2010, when South Africa hosted the World Cup, kulula ran a promotion offering a free flight to anyone with the same name as the president of FIFA, Sepp Blatter. The actual Sepp Blatter did not take them up on the offer, but a man named his dog Sepp Blatter to take advantage of the offer. Since the airline didn't specify that Sepp Blatter had to be a person, they were good sports, and hosted the Boston Terrier on several flights—and posted about it on Facebook.

But perhaps the most salient detail of "Flying 101" is that the idea for it came from a junior staff member at the airline. This is an airline that empowers its staff and rewards them for their efforts. The airline is in turn rewarded with employees who stay with the company for a long time. Cherese has been with the airline for seven years now, and while that's by no means a record for longevity at the company, hers is typical of the staff's loyalty to the brand. Management green-lighted her outside-the-box "Flying 101" idea when she was still a newbie, and they were rewarded for doing so when the photos of the plane went viral, proving that loyalty is a two-way street. As Cherese said, "Passion runs through the team." She added, "I still have fun with my own brand. That's why I love the kulula brand so much."

It should be noted that "Flying 101," along with a few other custom-painted planes (e.g., "This Way Up," with big arrows pointing in a skyward direction), were the exception rather than the rule. But the reason for this is not that the airline has become stodgier since "Flying 101." Instead, the reason is actually quite customer-centric. Iain Meaker, Executive Manager of Commercial Distribution, told us this about custom-designed aircraft: "It becomes extremely costly… every time there's a cutline, in terms of a change in color, it creates drag and resistance…. We could actually see the difference that [a custom-designed] aircraft had from a fuel efficiency perspective with another aircraft that was a lot more standard with regard to the paint schemes." The time and labor for the custom painting also added to the expense. So rather than raise the price of your ticket as costs for aircraft and fuel increase, kulula has opted for a simpler design to keep fares as low as possible. The opportunity for "Flying

101" arose partly because kulula at the time was buying used aircraft. They leveraged that brand opportunity well. Once they introduced their brand new fleet of Boeing 737-800s, painting was done at the Boeing factory and needed to be more streamlined. This meant that special liveries could only be done on a one-off basis. Though on the plus side, despite having a less quirky livery is that kulula has the youngest fleet of commercial aircraft in all of Southern Africa.

Now back to our flight. You board the aircraft and find your way to a seat, which you can either select on the spot upon checking in for your flight, or reserve 24 hours prior to your flight as well as the ability to pre-purchase your seat in advance. Again, if you're not used to flying, your nerves may be a little on edge, so you pick up the safety card in the seat pocket in front of you, and you're greeted by a photo of some friendly faces. Hey, one of those faces looks familiar. You look up and realize that the flight attendant in the photo on your safety card is the same person who greeted you when you boarded the plane. As Service Delivery Manager Tracey McCreadie told us, majority of the time when you see a picture of kulula staff on a billboard or a safety card, those are not models, they are actual kulula staff. Their families are very proud to see their faces representing the kulula brand, so this is another way the airline fosters loyalty among staff: they celebrate them, and let them know in myriad ways that they *are* the brand.

After that pleasant moment of recognition, you start to peruse the safety card, and more grinning ensues. You're looking at the drawings illustrating how to retrieve your life jacket from under your seat and put it on when you spot the caption, "Cool yellow jackets double up as funky retro-style fashion accessories." And then there's "This mysterious, yet amazing green line represents world peace... actually it's the illuminated emergency exit floor light showing the way out." Next to the picture showing how to position yourself in the unlikely event of a crash landing: "Only necessary if the 'brace' command is given... don't be a nana and do it every time someone sneezes..." And then of course there's "We really like these safety cards... they make great fanning devices, so please don't remove them from the airplane." If you are like many other passengers, you ignore this last little instruction and surreptitiously shove the safety card into your carry-on. Not to worry: kulula has anticipated your kleptomania—they always keep extras on board for the next flight.

When the safety announcement begins, and the flight attendants start demonstrating the procedures, you're dozing off, because you already memorized the safety card. But you're awakened when you hear the flight attendant say "For take-off and touchdown your tray tables will need to be folded away, seat in the most uncomfortable upright position, window blinds open and those seatbelts fastened tight around those gorgeous hips." Now that they've got your attention, you're hearing about "...the most appropriate brace position that you'd adopt in case of an emergency landing. This is when we all bend over and kiss our asses goodbye" (a verbatim quotation from a YouTube video recording a past safety announcement). The very thing that you thought an airline would never joke about—passenger safety—is peppered with jokes. The airline is, of course, very serious about safety. Tracey McCreadie told us that in the two-and-a-half months it takes to train new cabin crew, more time is spent drilling them on safety than anything else. But kulula is aware of the fact that laughter relaxes the body, and is therefore a potent antidote to anxiety. It's a fine balance, of course. They can't make fun of the safety measures themselves—if you peruse the safety card or watch the popular YouTube video of the kulula flight attendant giving safety instructions, you will see that the comedy not only does not interfere with the delivery of this most important kind of information; rather, it actually enhances the delivery by drawing passengers' attention toward a part of the flight that many of us usually tune out.

The Emotional Side of Flying

The way kulula used comedy in the early days of the brand, and the way that use of comedy has evolved as the brand has matured, speaks volumes about how well the airline understands their customers' psychological relationship to flying. Shaun Pozyn, who runs kulula's marketing, said, "Essentially, if you look at it in its basic format, we are an airline, and we're in the transport business. But we've always looked to the emotional side. What does it mean to be flying? It's about connecting people, whether it's a guy returning from college for the holidays, whether it's lovers getting together from a long distance relationship... it's about the whole South African flame of people always being together and celebrating."

Our conversation with Tracey McCreadie, who hires and manages all of kulula's cabin crew, amply demonstrated the many ways kulula looks to the emotions not only of its passengers, but its employees as well. Tracey herself started as a flight attendant in 1997, so she living proof of the airline's effectiveness in creating staff loyalty. And since she understands the job from the inside out, she is also now building that loyalty in new generations of cabin crewmembers, as well as teaching them how to cultivate loyalty among customers.

The hiring process itself is very rigorous. Recruitment of any given member of the cabin crew takes four to six months. Once they are hired there's a two-and-a-half-month training program. The abundance of time that is devoted to the recruiting stage should give you an idea of just how selective kulula is about whom they hire to take care of their passengers in the air. They are looking for employees with great people skills, of course, but people skills come in more than one flavor and kulula is particular about theirs. The airline is owned by Comair, which also has a licensing agreement with British Airways PLC in South Africa, and the two airlines recruit from the same applicant pool. As Tracey said, "We've got two brands. One is very traditional, formal… And the other one is more relaxed and a lot of fun." Until recent years, each airline had its own cabin crew that it did not share with the other. The people who tended to be more extroverted were sent to kulula, while the quieter, more formal types were sent to British Airways. Nowadays, the two airlines share cabin crew, so flight attendants have to be flexible as to how many watts of personality to turn on, depending on which uniform they're wearing.

And as the kulula brand has matured, cabin crew have had to learn to modify their wattage even from one kulula flight to another. kulula has increasingly become the airline of choice not only for holidaymakers, but also for business travelers on routes like Johannesburg to Cape Town. Several of the people we spoke to at kulula told us that on the whole they've dialed the slapstick down to accommodate the businesspeople, who may want to focus on their laptop screens rather than getting a proverbial pie in the face. But according to Tracey, how much metaphorical pie to throw is something the crew has to gauge for themselves, from flight to flight. One of the important jobs of a kulula cabin controller is to look at the passengers on any given flight, take a reading of them, and communicate to their crew: "Okay, there are a lot of business passengers on this flight so ease up on the schtick," or, "These are mostly holidaymakers so you can be a little looser on this flight." The adaptive nature of each flight allows the passengers to be more comfortable with the style of service too.

If you are a kulula passenger, you may not know that this calculation is happening on every flight, but you will feel its effects. You will be grateful that the crew hired to take care of you while you're in the confined space of a flying machine for several hours is empathetic and sensitive to your needs.

Tuning into the passengers' needs doesn't stop at deciding how many jokes to tell. Let's say, for example, that you're a mother flying with an infant. Suddenly the thing you most fear happens: Your infant starts to wail. Tracey says, "We tell our crew, 'Look at how the mother is feeling. The mother is sitting in the cabin, and she's anxious because the baby is making a lot of noise. She's not able to calm the baby. If you start offering assistance to her, she's going to open up to you.' So it's having that empathy for the person to say, 'In that situation, the woman is feeling uncomfortable. Let me take her to an area, if the seatbelt signs are off, where there's a bit more space, a bit more privacy.' And then you can start engaging and talking to the passenger. Of course, if the seatbelt signs are on, then you stay in that area and you offer assistance. You also try to calm the mother down because the mother will often be panicking, which then sets the child often to scream a lot more." Another strategy Tracey suggests: "Sometimes it's good to take the baby away from the parents for a few minutes just so the parents can have something cold to drink, calm down a little bit, feel more relaxed. And the flight attendant is not so stressed, so the baby can settle quite easily."

If you are that mother on the flight, you are going to feel very grateful to the flight attendant who went out of their way to help you and your baby. Well beyond price, that is the kind of interaction with the brand that will induce your loyalty. There are a number of airlines that now have professionally trained flying nannies, like Etihad Airways or Air New Zealand; kulula is not there yet. At the same time, a large majority of airlines treat crying infants as a nuisance, and that's where kulula comes out on top.

There is another important loyalty issue worth bringing up here. It is obvious that kulula expects its crew to deliver a very high level of service. But how does the brand reward crewmembers and other employees for performing so consistently well, such that they will want to continue working for the company, as for example Tracey herself has done for almost 20 years now?

When we asked Comair's CEO Erik Venter why so many people stay with the airline for so long, he said, "I think a lot of it has to do with the fact that we come from a small family business, where everybody knew everybody else." Now, even though kulula's parent company, Comair, has a profit of 373 million South African rand (about US$28 million) on revenues of 6.3 billion rands in 2014, kulula has retained that family ethos. "So it's still very much an open-door type of family culture in the business," Erik said. "And once people get into that, they don't really want to go into a typical corporate culture after that." A case in point would be the Cherese "Flying 101" story. The new kid in the design department comes up with an idea that will cost the company a lot of money, but they try it anyway.

Management's support for employees is a company-wide philosophy. Tracey says, "We stress a lot with our cabin crew management that they have to be there for the cabin crew. Crew need that affirmation and appreciation. And when you give that to them, then they pass that on to their passengers. So that's a massive thing within our management structure."

Speaking of empathy, Tracey herself shows her roots as a flight attendant in the way she demonstrates empathy for the flight attendants she is now in charge of: "And you must also remember the cabin attendant's lifestyle; they have no control over what's happening. I will tell them what the roster is going to look like, where they will be flying, who they will be flying with. And if they come to work tomorrow, and I canceled one flight, I can put them on another flight. So they have very little control in the planning of their lives." She does as much as she can to offset the unpredictability of her team's lives by restoring some control to them where she can. "If they need a day off, or they need assistance with something, or a roster change, or a swap, we don't limit those things, because we want to make their lives as nice as possible." In any given three-month period, she will allow up to 20 percent of crewmembers to work on flights with other crewmembers they are friends with. After those three months are up, another, different 20 percent of the crew can fly with their friends. This freedom to choose workmates improves morale, and also tends to create good work chemistry on the flight as a whole.

Because kulula's brand identity relies so heavily on how the cabin crew interacts with the passengers—running the spectrum from upbeat and zany to compassionate and tender, as we have seen—staff morale is a huge component of kulula's brand. Or, as Tracey puts it, "We spend a hell of a lot of time and effort on keeping the crew happy." Managers will come in early and serve popcorn to the crew. Or they'll serve hot chocolate in winter or ice cream in summer. In the past, kulula has paired up with a spa to give crew-members foot massages twice a month just before they embark on a flight or just after they land. In the flight attendants' lounge, there is a "brag board" where people can post notes about things they have done well or have been complimented on.

Moreover, there are a number of peer leadership teams in which team members are empowered to come up with ideas and pursue initiatives that in other companies would be the domain of management. There is a grooming committee, for example, that creates the rules and standards for how people are required to look when they show up for work. And there is a "think vision" team that is responsible for coming up with strategies for improving service. The fact that these guidelines and initiatives are coming from their peers rather than from their managers inspires other crewmembers to take pride in their performance. This is how *esprit de corps*, or team spirit, is built at kulula.

Another way that Tracey motivates the crew can be summed up in one word: swag. A company will approach the kulula marketing department with a sponsorship deal that would involve crewmembers promoting that company's product on board. "And I'm the biggest pain… because [I ask], what is my crew getting for this?" For instance, a company wanted the crew to do a kind of live advertisement for their product during flights. So Tracey arranged for the company to give free samples to any crewmembers who were involved in the campaign. Then, when it came time for the crewmember to pitch the product, they were willing to do it enthusiastically because they were able to speak from experience having sampled the product themselves.

The crewmembers who participate in promotions like this will also report back to management about how successful it was, so even as they are pitching the product, they are also collecting useful data that kulula management can report back to the sponsor. In fact, crewmembers are relied upon to be the eyes and ears for the success of the kulula product as well. They are often the first to know if some particular aspect of kulula's service is successful or unsuccessful, because they hear about it from passengers in the normal course of their work. This makes the cabin crew a critical channel through which passengers can communicate with kulula's management.

Tracey summed up the interdependency of the company, the employees, and the customers as follows: "If my management team looks after my staff, and my staff will look after our passengers, and then our passengers will look after the shareholders, and the shareholders, in return, will look after the company, then we can make profits and pay our bonuses and everything."

Onward and Upward

Let us return once again to our quintessential kulula passenger. After a mirth-filled flight, the plane lands in Johannesburg. The pilot of this domestic South African carrier announces over the PA, "Welcome to Zimbabwe!" And then a few last jokes from the flight attendant before you depart: "When you leave the aircraft please take all your personal belongings with you except for the expensive stuff—cameras, laptops, et cetera—will be divided up among the crew."

And so ends your surprisingly memorable flight on kulula. But that is not necessarily the end of your experience of the brand. At this stage of its development, kulula is not just an airline. Through partnerships with other travel-related companies, as Shaun Pozyn says, "kulula no longer offers just flights, but an array of travel-related products including hotel accommodation, car hire, as well as holiday packages, both internationally and domestically."

The airline has acknowledged that business travelers are now a substantial part of its customer base by offering special deals for businesses. While kulula is still very much a people's airline—no business class seats or premium lounge—they offer large corporate clients and small and medium-sized businesses something called a BizDeal, predicated on the fact that business flyers are more prone to changing their flights. Thus, this deal offers the flexibility corporate clients require. And one of the major South African health insurers, Discovery Health, offers up to a 35 percent discount on kulula tickets to eligible members of their loyalty program, Vitality, which rewards people with a proven record of being healthy and fit.

The future for kulula is to continue to provide inexpensive air travel, great value, and their own quirky brand of exuberance, while tailoring the experience more and more to individual customers. With access to more refined data for every passenger, the airline hopes to offer a unique experience to each person based on their specific history, interests, and needs. This could include anything from when your wedding anniversary is, to the traffic you're likely to encounter on the way to the airport, to your interest in sports cars, to the fact that the flight attendant spilled coffee on your pants the last time you flew with the airline.

kulula is not the only airline in the world that is looking toward using refined data to personalize a passenger's experience, but the goal fits especially well with kulula's brand identity as a people-centric airline.

6X Analysis

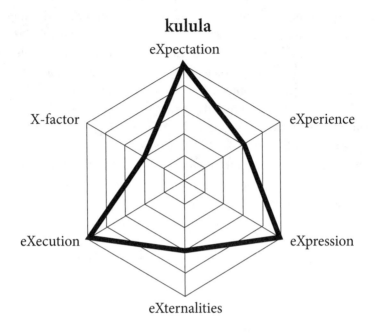

kulula

eXpectation

eXperience

eXpression

eXternalities

eXecution

X-factor

kulula hits the mark on just about every facet of **eXpectation**. They are human, down-to-earth, and people-friendly in the brand image they project. The fact that they use actual flight attendants in most of their advertising gives the brand a strong feeling of authenticity. The folksy humor of their billboards, radio, and TV spots resonates strongly with potential customers. And they are consistent. Though the airline has muted the wackiness factor a little bit in deference to their business travelers, they can still be relied upon to make passengers laugh before, during, and after a flight.

Brand **eXpression** is particularly strong with respect to empowering staff. They are given a lot of leeway to handle issues with passengers as they see fit, and they are amply rewarded for taking initiative—Cherese Wansink's "Flying 101" plane is a perfect example. Feedback loops—both between passengers and staff and among staff—are abundant. Crewmembers and other staff who interface with customers are encouraged to seek feedback from customers on all aspects of their experience, and managers likewise are highly motivated to keep tabs on what their teams need and how best to assist them in their work.

Internal brand resonance is the standout component of kulula's **eXecution**, as proven by people like Brian Kitchin, who started as a ramp agent and is now Executive Manager of Sales, or Tracey McCreadie, who went from flight attendant to Service Delivery Manager. Brag boards, foot massages, or scheduling accommodations all make coming to work more pleasant and interesting. Putting non-managerial staff on committees normally filled by executives lets them know that internally as well as externally, kulula is a people's airline.

6: SINGAPORE AIRLINES: NO DETAIL TOO SMALL

A Near Miss

It was a sunny morning in Tokyo. I strolled out of my hotel in a relaxed state, on schedule to arrive at Tokyo-Narita Airport in plenty of time to catch my flight back to Singapore. I was excited, as it was my first-ever flight on Singapore Airlines—an airline I had always heard so much about. When I reached the train station in downtown Tokyo I discovered that a ticket to Narita Airport cost 500 yen more than I had in my pocket at the time. Now slightly less relaxed, I hustled out of the station, found a currency exchange facility, changed my U.S. dollars into yen, hustled back, and jumped on the next train. Okay, I thought, minor glitch, I'm cutting it a bit close, but I'll still be there on time. However, I arrived at the Narita Airport station only to discover that the distance I had to walk—make that *run*—from the station to the airport was much farther than I'd anticipated. I wasn't so relaxed when I finally got to the terminal and saw on the flight information screens that it was time for the final boarding of my Singapore flight. I scanned the terminal for the Singapore Airlines (SIA) counter and couldn't find it. In desperation, I went to Air

France, the closest counter to me, and they told me all SIA counters were closed. I had two bags to check, my flight was about to depart, and my relaxation had already departed.

I raced to the airport information desk and asked them to call someone from SIA. Within minutes, a young woman wearing the SIA lanyard came running toward me. Based on less-than-pleasant experiences with other airlines, I expected her to greet me with at least a telltale raised eyebrow, maybe some disapproving words, and quite possibly an unapologetic shrug. Instead, to my surprise, she glanced at my ticket and said calmly and without judgment, "Mr. Nigam, you're very late, our check-in counters are closed, but let me see what I can do." She immediately radioed the staff at the gate and asked them to print my boarding pass. Then she grabbed one of my bags and asked me to follow her. She led me at a fast clip to the express lane at security, where she helped expedite the scanning of my bags, including my large check-in bags, and then we rushed on toward the gate. Before we got there, we were met by a young man from SIA who handed me my boarding pass, took both my bags, and sprinted with them the rest of the distance to the gate. He tagged my larger bag and gave it to the baggage handlers, who took it directly from the gangway to the plane's cargo hold. Breathless, I stepped on board the Boeing 747, where a flight attendant greeted me with the customary, soft-voiced "Welcome aboard, Mr. Nigam." And I was flying in economy class, for the first time with this airline. I was amazed.

The way I was treated upon my late arrival for this flight gets right to the heart of SIA's success as a brand. As we all know, airline travel can be unpredictable and unsettling. Maybe, as happened to me, you don't have enough cash in the right currency to pay for your train ticket to the airport. Or maybe you take a taxi and get stuck in a monster traffic jam. Or your taxi takes you to the wrong terminal, or you drive your own car but your parking lot is full. Bad weather, flight delays, lost passport, lost luggage, a colicky baby in the seat behind you. The list of things that can go wrong on an airplane voyage is nearly endless. At the core of SIA's brand is their ability, despite the potential chaos, to deliver a predictable, orderly, and, above all, comforting experience, in which you the passenger feel that your needs are always the priority of all airline personnel you encounter.

In this way, SIA has set the gold standard in the industry for the overall travel experience, now emulated by many other airlines. This standard is achieved through the airline's three-pronged focus on making the customer feel important, offering a highly consistent flying experience and rigorously training their crew.

All three of these ingredients were at work on the day I was late for my flight from Tokyo to Singapore. The crew who helped me make it to my flight acted as if getting me on that plane before the gate closed was their top priority at that moment. They made me feel important without judging me or sending me on a guilt-trip for being so delayed. As for consistency, whatever stress my delay may have caused them, they presented the same demeanor passengers have come to expect from SIA staff: cheerful, calm, eager to serve. And their training was evident in the instantaneous, unfaltering, seamless way they worked together to solve my problem. As you will see in this chapter, SIA braids together these three strategies through every touch point of passenger engagement.

The Making of a Singapore Girl

As SIA's instantly recognizable brand ambassador, she *is* the X-factor—that special something that no other airline can replicate. As we will discuss in detail below, other airlines have worked hard to imitate various aspects of SIA's outstanding service formula, but no one else has the Singapore Girl.

We had the good fortune to sit down with flight attendant Michelle Ong, who told us the story of her life as a Singapore Girl.

When she was 12 or 13 years old, years before her first SIA job interview in 2007, she used to go to the airport in Singapore to pick up her father when he returned from business trips. Even then, she remembers seeing the Singapore Girls walking through the airport in their uniform, the signature Sarong Kebaya, with their perfectly coiffed hair and their unmistakable poise. Her dream of joining the airline began then. You won't often spot an actual airplane in SIA's advertising campaigns, but you will always see the Singapore Girl. She is the airline's most important brand icon.

Michelle was just 21, a student finishing her university degree when she heard SIA was holding flight attendant interviews. Her interview was scheduled the day before a final paper was due, but she went anyway, embracing her destiny.

As Singapore Airlines CEO Goh Choon Phong pointed out when we spoke with him, the selection process for flight attendants is very rigorous, particularly now when the culture in Singapore and elsewhere in Asia is changing. Younger generations of both men and women are placing a higher value on individuality than their forebears. The airline's Assistant Manager of Cabin Crew Training, Foo Juat Fang, adds that the Singapore economy is very different today than it was in 1977, when she herself started work as a Singapore Girl. Singapore had achieved independence as a nation in 1965, and far fewer jobs were available. Flight attendants were happy to have a steady paycheck, and to be able to fly to so many of the places around the world that they had studied about in school. The current generation has a much greater selection of jobs available to them, and many more opportunities to travel abroad before they reach the age when they have to work.

And so, particularly these days, SIA is looking for someone like Michelle, who already has an affinity with SIA. New employees are chosen not only for their willingness to embrace the service ethos that SIA passengers have come to expect over the decades, but also for their appreciation of the value of working together with a team of fellow employees all dedicated to the goal of excellence. Of the 1000 or so people who come for each walk-in interview session in Singapore, fewer than 100 are chosen on average. There are more than six such sessions held each year. Michelle claims to have been very shy before she started with the airline, but her interviewers, who were themselves seasoned flight supervisors, must have seen a quality in her that she may not have been aware she possessed. Applicants are evaluated not just for intelligence, which is an important part of the job, but for emotional intelligence as well, which is equally indispensable. Since being a flight attendant is an inherently social job, group interviews are a crucial part of the selection process—the interviewers are looking for how applicants interact with one another. Supervisors will even observe the applicants when they are waiting to be interviewed, to get a sense of how they behave when they don't know they're being watched.

Michelle got the job, and she remembers with excitement the rite of passage of being fitted for her custom-tailored Sarong Kebaya. The distinctive uniform, created by couture designer Pierre Balmain, is so iconic that in 1993, Madame Tussauds' Wax Museum in London made a wax figure of the Singapore Girl, their first-ever figure representing a commercial enterprise.

As we have learned from Michelle, and from our own experience flying the airline, the soft, deferential appearance—and, indeed, the word "Girl"—belie the intense and rigorous undertaking of being an SIA flight attendant. Not to mention that these days a full 40 percent of SIA cabin crew are men. Regardless of gender, the job requires tremendous intelligence, commitment, skill, self-control, flexibility, and hard work. As the airline's Senior Vice President of Product and Services Marvin Tan shared, the inherent challenge of anyone working as a flight attendant is that their job takes place in "a very confined space with very limited resources at their disposal."

Training

The training program for new crew members is 15 weeks long. This training period—the longest in the industry—is overseen by a team of in-house facilitators as well as external consultants. The airline's training school is a recognized training organization under a collaboration with the Singapore Workforce Development Agency and offers accredited courses. They teach new arrivals everything from how to serve a meal to how to handle a medical emergency. In order that the service not be carried out by rote, but with genuine feeling, trainees are provided detailed rationales for everything they do. As Juat Fang shared, attention to detail is implicit and integral to service excellence and is emphasized repeatedly during training. Ensuring that the SIA logo on the serviceware always faces the passenger is one example, and is part and parcel of SIA's brand reinforcement. When a flight attendant on SIA places a cup on a passenger's tray table, the only audience for that logo is the passenger, but it is a subtle reminder that you will be exceedingly well taken care of on that flight.

Perhaps even more important than procedure, trainers also transmit the culture and values of the airline, which happen to align with the traditional culture and values of Asian hospitality. Important markets for SIA include China, India, Japan, and Southeast Asian nations like Indonesia. The airline's practices appeal especially to travelers from these countries, which prize values like respect for elders.

Giving older, longtime employees a revered status within the airline is an important feature of internal brand building. The older generation takes pride in what they've accomplished during their tenure at SIA. That pride is reinforced by their status at the airline as revered elders, and they in turn inculcate that sense of pride in the younger generation. In this process, positive feelings about the brand are developed among new employees and reinforced among the seasoned ones.

Over past few decades, the brand of the Singapore Girl has only become stronger as it stands out against a plethora of new airlines cropping up in the region. The Singapore Girl's consistency in service delivery is unmatched. Frequent flier Khoa Huynh shared with us, "Consistency of service delivery is paramount to the Singapore Airlines brand and I always call it out when it is not. When you fly Singapore Airlines, particularly in business, first or suites, you do expect perfection. It is a brand I can rely on." So how did SIA manage to maintain the brand consistency over generations? That is a challenge, since the characteristics of the crew being hired have evolved over time.

Juat Fang talked with us about how training, too, has evolved in the nearly 40 years she's been with the airline. Her initial training, she said, lasted only four weeks, and she learned how to serve in both economy class and first class on one aircraft, the Boeing 707. Later, she went on to receive additional training for other aircraft in the fleet. Now, the new crew are trained for two different types of aircraft, but the initial training focuses on only economy-class service. In the 70s, Juat Fang told us, most crew came from larger families with relatively more siblings, and naturally would have had more experience in caring for others. These days, new employees are more likely to come from smaller families with less experience and exposure to caretaking.

As Juat Fang said, "In the early days if you asked someone to jump, they said 'How high?' Today if you ask the younger crowd to jump, they say 'Why?'" So part of what the long training accomplishes is an acclimation to and an embracing of the airline's core values of service, excellence, and teamwork. As Marvin said, "It might sound like an oxymoron but we need our crew to have both pride and humility."

An example of how pride and humility come together is the famous Sarong Kebaya itself. Michelle is not unusual among new recruits who have been drawn to work for SIA because they've been exposed to images of the Singapore Girl throughout their lives, and would be proud to become one. They want to wear the uniform, have the look, have the elegant bearing. Michelle was so over-the-moon when her uniform arrived from the tailors that she couldn't sleep that whole night. Still, if you're used to wearing jeans and a t-shirt, and then you put on the custom-made SIA uniform with its fitted long skirt, you have to learn how to walk with a shorter stride and sit elegantly. Even bending over to pick up a fallen object—not an unheard-of part of a flight attendant's job—requires the modern-day Singapore Girl to learn a whole new set of dance moves. This may not come naturally to modern young women. Some of them initially bristle, even ones who like the idea of wearing the beautiful uniform. Yet, if they're committed to the endeavor, then they come to welcome this physical adjustment as one of the rigors of being part of a team they can be proud of.

Still More Training

The training does not stop at 15 weeks, either. In fact, it never really stops. Before every flight, the crew gets together for a briefing. At this pre-flight session, crewmembers will share experiences and key learning points, talking about how they effectively solved problems that may have arisen on flights, to celebrate their achievements, to inspire one another, and to learn from one another's successes. This sharing is a critical part of the airline culture that fosters peer-to-peer learning and instills pride among crew in working for SIA.

Crewmembers are also invited to comment on one another's performance via an electronic Cabin Crew Development Form (CCDF). Michelle told us of a very positive CCDF she and her colleagues received for their handling of a tricky situation. In the middle of a flight, a passenger soiled his pants. Michelle immediately got him a towel and some blankets, and escorted him to the bathroom to clean himself up. In the mean time she and her colleagues used products and equipment they had on board to clean and dry his seat by the time he returned. From the moment Michelle discovered the problem until it was resolved, all crewmembers involved recognized the importance of being discreet and maintaining a cheerful facial expression and supportive demeanor, so as few other passengers as possible would know of this passenger's difficulties, and the passenger himself would feel cared for rather than judged or shamed by the crew. What could have been a disastrous flying experience for the incontinent passenger and those near him became an opportunity for Michelle and the crew to deliver a positive SIA brand experience to them. And that in turn became an opportunity for their colleagues to appreciate and reward their quick thinking and their efforts.

Michelle says the training and the years of experience on the job have changed her for the better as a person. When she started working as a flight attendant, her natural shyness made her feel overwhelmed at having to interact with so many passengers. But the training, both in advance and on the job, has enabled her to become more relaxed and at ease in social encounters of all kinds. "Even my mom is amazed!" she said.

Part of the ongoing training is the rigorous program of reviews that each crewmember undergoes. A new crewmember's in-flight performance is monitored and reviewed by a supervisor eight times in the first six months. Thereafter, each crewmember receives a thorough onboard assessment six times a year.

Finally, once or twice a year, people in management positions in the airline serve as crewmembers. Even the CEO Goh Choon Phong does not get a pass on this one. He sits in on the pre-flight crew briefing, and pays attention as senior crewmembers offer service tips for this particular set of passengers going to this destination. As Choon Phong said when we talked, when he serves on a flight crew he becomes rookie for a day among the professional, highly trained staff. Given his relative inexperience, he is not given the full complement of duties on board. "I do the simple stuff. I try to avoid the hot stuff, but serving ice cream is fine." Just as a novice flight attendant would be, seasoned supervisors make sure he does not cause any deterioration in the service experience of any passenger. This unique practice wherein SIA executives participate as flight crew fosters respect among management for the extremely rigorous nature of the flight crews' jobs. This also fosters a sense among the crew that management respects the crew's contribution to the airline and takes it very seriously.

Consistency and the Importance of the Passenger

The function of the unusually rigorous training SIA employees undergo is to ensure a consistent brand experience —especially on the day of travel. What remains consistent across all SIA flights is the passenger's sense of being exceptionally well taken care of.

Again, the Singapore Girl is central to these two features of SIA's identity, consistency and passenger importance. It is ultimately the superlative performance of her job, and not her recognizable appearance, that makes the Singapore Girl SIA's brand icon. However, since her appearance is a core component of the visual identity of the brand, it is not insignificant either. In addition to the custom-tailored Sarong Kebaya, flight attendants receive meticulous training as to how to do their hair and makeup. Juat Fang told us the makeup is calibrated so finely that the female cabin crew will adjust their make-up intensity based on whether it is a day or night flight.

Michelle amusedly describes being approached in an airport by an awed passenger who said, "Do you guys have personal hair stylists?" The answer is no, but flight attendants often do their grooming together—which can take about an hour each time!—to make sure they are all meeting the same high standard for their appearance.

The consistency of their appearance is, in a sense, a promise that consistency will extend into passenger service, and it does. When speaking with passengers, flight attendants are mindful that their tone, volume, and even their cadence are congruent with the sense of trust and safety established. With a timid or sleeping passenger, Juat Fang says, a soft, gentle tone and manner of speaking are encouraged. Where appropriate, the attendant will stoop or kneel so as to be at eye level when interacting with the passenger. If a passenger happens to be sleeping when the plane is about to land at its destination, the attendant will tell them so in a whisper.

The soft voice, the lowering of the body, these are specifically Asian forms of hospitality. If you are a western reader, you may be thinking at this point, isn't the deference excessive? If the majority of passengers on SIA flights were American or European, the deferential Asian approach to hospitality would not be as relevant to them, and would not have the same kind of cultural resonance. But since the passengers within SIA's crucial eight-hour flying radius comprise a substantial proportion of Chinese, Japanese, Indonesian, and Indian travelers, the Singapore Girl's demeanor is intended to help them feel at ease. Japanese passengers are known to be hard to impress, but seeing a flight attendant lowering her body to address them at eye level makes them feel more at home. Interestingly, the western passengers who are loyal to SIA often cite this very demeanor, which they seldom find in a home airline, as their reason for preferring to fly SIA.

And again it's worth pointing out that the Singapore Girl's quiet demeanor is undergirded by skill and strength. One SIA flight from Singapore to London made the headlines in 2013 because during breakfast service, the aircraft abruptly experienced moderate to severe turbulence, and the food went flying everywhere. Eleven passengers and one crewmember sustained minor injuries. If they were shaken up, the crew didn't show it. They cleaned up the mess and calmed everyone's nerves as quickly and efficiently as they could, and covered up the floor with blankets to prevent further injury. All passengers received boxes of chocolates when they disembarked in London.

Michelle says that when she started working at SIA, she was quite frightened by turbulence, but knew that her job was to provide an orderly experience to travelers in the midst of the unpredictability of air travel, even bad weather. She needed not only to present a calm face to passengers, but also to manage her own emotional distress so that she had the presence of mind to scan the cabin to see which passengers needed extra care during the bumps. Singapore Girls have often been likened to geishas, but, given the steely strength required for the job, one might equally liken them to samurai.

Another element of warm hospitality: Passengers are always addressed by name in the premium classes. Once I was boarding a SIA flight from New York to Frankfurt. I dropped my bag at my seat and headed directly to the restroom. On my way there, a flight attendant said to me, "Oh, Mr. Nigam, may I hang up your coat?" She knew my name without having seen which seat I was assigned to! Later in the flight I asked her how she'd managed this. She replied that since I was the last passenger to board the plane, she'd deduced my name by process of elimination. Okay, so she turns out not to have had supernatural powers, but her ability to produce my name on cue in this circumstance bespeaks alertness, quick thinking, a remarkably thorough knowledge of the passenger manifest, and of course, the desire and motivation to make me feel special.

The goal of the Singapore Girl is to be proactive. If a water glass is less than half full, they fill it before the passengers ask for it. On an overnight flight, they ask if passengers want their bed linens turned down. On other airlines you may see two or more flight attendants sitting or standing in the galley, chatting with each other or reading a magazine. On SIA that would never happen. There is an internal policy of "see-and-be-seen." Flight attendants are in the aisles for much of the flight both so that they can anticipate passengers' needs even before they arise, and so that passengers will have the sense that the attendants are always there when they need them. The cabin crew does their best to stay ahead of what is known as the Christmas-tree-lights effect, where multiple call buttons are illuminated up and down the cabin. That is a phenomenon you seldom see on an SIA flight. Michelle says that during pre-flight briefings, crewmembers are given specific targets to achieve for the flight. Regular cabin presence and prompt responses are some examples of targets which help in anticipating passengers' needs in advance, hence reducing the need for passengers to press the call button.

My own experience corroborates the proactive approach Michelle describes. On one SIA flight, as I was walking to the restroom after dinner, a flight attendant asked me if I'd like my bed made for the night. The following morning, moments after I woke up, another flight attendant offered me a wet towel to freshen up. Moments later, yet another came by to take my coffee order and provide me with glass of juice. Later, before I could even press the call button to say that my headphones were not working, a Singapore Girl was at my side with a new pair.

Again, things have changed over the years with respect to the see-and-be-seen policy. In the old days, on a long flight, there was one in-flight movie available, and it was played three times in succession. Having seen the movie once, a passenger would have a lot of time to kill, so flight attendants made a point of engaging in extended conversations with the customers. Back then, as Juat Fang put it, "We were the in-flight entertainment. Crew were actively and proactively keeping the passengers engaged through conversations, especially on the long-hauls, to keep their boredom at bay as the in-flight entertainment system back then was rudimentary." And of course there was more happening than just an enjoyable conversation. During these interactions, cabin crew were getting to know their passengers better to serve them even more effectively in the future.

When problems arise, the job of the crew is to handle them in a way that makes the customer feel taken care of. If the problem is directly or indirectly caused by the airline, the employee assumes responsibility. For example, if the in-flight entertainment system doesn't work, the customer is offered a seat change, and if that's not possible, or the flight is full, they're given an in-flight voucher. If a flight attendant cannot immediately resolve a problem, they will call upon an in-flight supervisor, who, even if the airline is not responsible for the problem, will always try to find a solution, or at least a compromise, all with a smiling face and cheerful demeanor.

Of course SIA is not the only airline that has consistently high standards for service, but other airlines approach things differently. Southwest, for example, prides itself on the individuality of its cabin crew, and flight attendants are encouraged to allow their idiosyncratic personalities to shine in their interactions with customers. This works well in the American market because the United States is a country that provides itself on what President Theodore Roosevelt referred to as "rugged individualism." Though things have been changing recently in Asia, there is still a greater emphasis there on collectivity.

However, Choon Phong is quick to point out that the consistency on which SIA prides itself is a consistency in excellent care, and does *not* mean a robotic approach to customer service, in which all passengers are treated identically. So, for example, not only do flight attendants know each business and first class passenger's name, but starting in 2011, SIA began work on a database about their passengers that employees across all touchpoints can both access and contribute to, which will help all of them give passengers personalized care. Flight attendants have access to the database, called the customer experience management (CEM) system, through a handheld device while they're on board the aircraft, and can update it with any new, relevant information they obtain on the flight. So while a long conversation between passengers and crew is less likely to happen on a 21st-century SIA flight than a 20th-century one, the modern high-tech flight attendant can compensate for the loss with this new way of gathering information.

The kind of information stored in the CEM system might be that Passenger A likes to be attended to multiple times during a flight, but Passenger B prefers to be left in peace. Passenger C likes coffee while Passenger D prefers green tea before landing, so without their having to ask for it, those drinks will be offered to those passengers during beverage service. This is a positive use of technology in which the machine is not introduced to take the place of the human worker, but rather to empower the worker to do the job they are motivated to do, which is to deliver a highly specific and individualized level of care on their flights. Choon Phong makes clear that flight attendants are very careful not to use the CEM system in any way that would make passengers feel threatened or intruded upon by the technology. For example, as a passenger you're unlikely to ever see a Singapore Girl looking up information about you, since the handheld devices are discreetly consulted in the galley. Moreover, only information relevant to taking the best care of each customer is entered into the database, nothing more.

Virgin Atlantic tried to use technology in a similar way, with less favorable results. They equipped their upper-class check-in staff with Google Glass, so that they could see information about each customer as that customer approached the check-in counter. At the time, Google Glass was newly on the market, and most customers hadn't seen one before, so they wanted to try it. As soon as they put it on, they saw that all the information about them that the check-in person had called up. Customers were creeped out by that, so the Google Glass initiative remained an experiment limited to London Heathrow. "You will never see Google Glass on our cabin crew, that's for sure," Choon Phong said.

If there's a way for SIA employees to go above and beyond even the expected high standards of care, they are encouraged to do it. A modest example would be a passenger in a window seat who is drinking a lot on a flight and needs to make frequent trips to the restroom. That passenger and the people seated between him and the aisle will likely be discomforted by these frequent trips, so an SIA flight attendant in this circumstance will try to move the window-seat passenger to an aisle.

Going above and beyond can get more extravagant, too. On more than one occasion, SIA staff have facilitated a marriage proposal. In one famous instance, a young man contacted SIA and arranged for the cabin crew to hold up a series of posters, to be shown to the would-be fiancée in sequence, each one containing one word of the phrase "Will… you… marry… me?" Luckily for everyone involved, the woman said yes, and the crew then came down the aisle with cake and chilled champagne on a trolley, with dry ice producing a billowing smoke effect. SIA is not the only airline on which the cabin crew has facilitated a marriage proposal, but this crew put some creativity into it, to make it a particularly fun and joyful experience for the couple and for everyone else on board.

Beyond the Singapore Girl

The subtle, intricately detailed nature of the Singapore Girl's approach to service speaks to the SIA experience. But that experience extends beyond the cabin crew themselves. As I myself discovered when I almost missed that flight from Tokyo to Singapore, passenger engagement doesn't only mean what happens in the confines of the aircraft for the duration of the flight. The check-in staff, the gate staff, and the baggage handlers were all involved in my boarding that plane on time. Their ability to communicate quickly and effectively with each other, to work as a team, and to harmonize the sequence of their actions all contributed to getting this tardy passenger where he needed to go. And not just the cabin crew but employees all along the service chain can contribute to and view the information stored on each passenger in the CEM system. While it is true that the signature feature of the SIA brand is the passenger's interpersonal experience, other touchpoints—and there are many in the airline business—count too. One of my own personal favorite features of the SIA experience outside the flights themselves is the lounge for first-class and business-class passengers. In the last year, I've flown Air Canada to London's Heathrow Airport more than a half a dozen times. The Air Canada lounge is directly across the hall from the newly opened SIA lounge at Heathrow's Terminal 2, and I've found myself repeatedly gravitating toward the SIA lounge. My main reason is probably the food. They serve traditional Singaporean comfort food such as chicken rice and laksa noodles. But my lounge preference is also to do with the homey feel of the SIA facility. There are private pods if I need to get work done, spacious showers to freshen up before boarding the flight, and there's even green-tea–flavored ice cream! The décor is not ostentatious, they don't make a big deal out of it, but travel can be stressful, so you go to the SIA lounge because you know you'll find relaxation and relief there. The vibe in the lounge proves that the understated feeling of being taken care of is embodied not only in the SIA cabin crew but in the airport experience as well. This, too, is part of the consistency and passenger-centric approach that is fundamental to SIA's brand identity. Rating websites like LoungeReview.com give five stars out of five to Singapore Airline's lounges at both Heathrow and in Singapore.

Other airlines are competing to offer passengers a level of premium service comparable to or exceeding that of SIA and some have tried their own innovations. But time and time again, SIA beats the competition in consistent excellence. Unlike SIA, Emirates offers showers on their flights, but only on their A380 aircraft, not on the 777s. Etihad keeps up reasonably well with SIA's service standard in first and business classes, but is inconsistent in economy. For regional flights, Qatar Airways will sometimes put passengers, without telling them, on a smaller single-class A320 aircraft without embedded in-flight entertainment. Turkish Airlines has much to recommend them once they get you up in the air (see our chapter on this outstanding airline), but there's only so much they can do about the overcrowding of their hub airport, Istanbul. Robin Speculand, a top tier frequent flier with Singapore Airlines told us, "Other airlines now offer a comparable or better first-class lounge experience and work harder to be the best way to fly. I have been PPS Solitaire (highest level in the airline's frequent flier program) for over a decade now and they do excel in areas like their management of the call center. For example, if the phone is cut off they immediately call you back."

It is in orderliness and consistency—across all touchpoints, in the air and on the ground—that SIA prevails over the others. With their deep pockets, Emirates offers limousine service to its first-class and business-class passengers, while Qatar Airlines has swimming pools in its first-class lounge. Choon Phong is not interested in competing with such flashy innovations, but in expanding and improving in areas where SIA already excels.

One of these areas is its network of flights. In Southeast Asia, no other full-service airline can match the number of destinations to which SIA flies on a regular basis. This high level of connectivity is a brand promise SIA has no problem delivering on within their flying radius. But since it is simply not possible for any one airline to have that kind of reach throughout the world, SIA has made a point of partnering with full-service carriers in other countries, including Virgin Australia, Air New Zealand, and Lufthansa. So even if SIA does not fly directly to some of the smaller airports in Europe or Australia, they will offer seamless connectivity to those destinations thanks to their cooperative agreements with other carriers. And then there are the interior spaces of the SIA aircraft. As you would expect, given the meticulous attention paid to every other aspect of the flight experience, the décor of SIA aircraft is designed with an understated elegance and a functionality geared toward maximum ease and comfort of passengers. The SIA marketing department found an ingenious way to communicate this to fans and would-be SIA passengers: a video titled "No Detail Is Too Small" that is a perfect expression of the SIA brand, timed just after the launch of the premium-economy cabin aboard the airline.

The video was launched on YouTube and social media in December of 2015, and as of this writing it has had more than 1.6 million views. It shows an astonishingly intricate miniature model of SIA's A380 being constructed by the American artist Luca Iaconi-Stewart entirely out of carefully cut-up manila folders. Iaconi-Stewart had made a similar model of an Air India 777 in 2014, but the quintessential SIA twist was to create a making-of video. You see him cutting 3,000 tiny pieces of manila folder and then assembling them into all the interior cabin features of the A380, including chairs that recline in economy, premium economy, and business class, and, in first class, chairs that transform into beds and sliding doors that can be closed to create private sleeping compartments. This gave SIA the opportunity to show off the beauty and comfort of their aircrafts' interior design, and to bring added awareness to the new premium economy seating they'd introduced earlier in the year. However, as we've said, branding is ultimately about a feeling, and the feeling you come away with after watching this video is very much in synergy with SIA's service ethos: literally thousands of little details have come together seamlessly to provide you with a rare level of ease and comfort when you fly this airline.

A Worst-Case Scenario

I'd like to end this chapter with what might strike you as a touching story, since I think it encapsulates SIA's unusual handling of crisis situations. The worst thing that can happen to an airline and to its passengers is for a plane to go down. This happened to SIA for the first time ever in 2000, when one of their Boeing 747s crashed on the runway in Taipei during takeoff. Of the 179 passengers and crew on board, there were a number of fatalities and severe injuries. SIA got off to a rocky start in their handling of communications about the accident when a Los Angeles spokesman told the press that no one on board had died. They were slow to release the names of the dead and wounded, so some people close to the passengers found out their loved ones had died from the news rather than the airline.

Into this truly painful situation stepped Rick Clements, then SIA's Vice President of Public Affairs, who held a press conference in Singapore. As Clements was discussing the compensation the airline would offer the families of the deceased and injured, an exhausted, distraught man shoved his way past security and demanded to know why he had first learned of his brother's death from the press and not from the airline. A security agent attempted to escort him away, but Clements asked that the man be allowed to stay and continue talking.

The bereaved man spoke for several minutes in front of TV cameras and reporters, looking exhausted and gasping for breath. "We want to know what really happened," he said. "All our news is from the newspaper reporter and you are the ones who tell me… not to believe the press."

Clements listened calmly to the man. He then stepped down off the stage and walked toward him. Clements looked him in the eyes, put his arm around him, and comforted him, all while cameras were rolling and press was watching. This went far beyond a PR man doing his job. This was one human being connecting with another at a very difficult time in the latter's life. Ultimately, when we entrust our time, ourselves, and our lives to an airline, we are looking not only for professional service, but also for a compassionate understanding of our needs as human beings. This difficult moment in the history of Singapore Airlines embodies that understanding.

In conclusion, Singapore Airlines will face increasing competitive pressures from the ever-improving Middle Eastern airlines at the high-end of the market, whereas the low-cost carriers will continue to attract regional traffic. To succeed in the long run, the airline needs to maintain a razor-sharp focus on the Singapore Girl, its network, and consistent service. Time and again externalities will test the airline, and Singapore Airlines will need to be consistent in displaying its human side to win hearts.

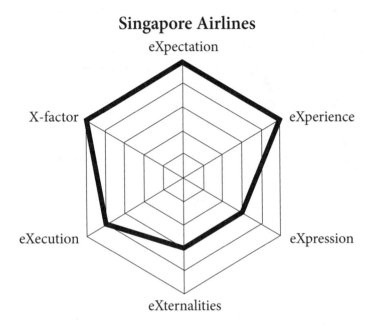

Singapore Airlines

Singapore Airlines relies on an unwavering dedication to excellence, delivered by a rigorously trained crew, to provide a uniquely consistent brand **eXperience** to passengers. The SIA experience has remained remarkably consistent over time, and that's been the airline's competitive advantage. SIA passengers expect a minimum level of service every single time they fly and the airline seldom disappoints. That's why they keep coming back.

In this endeavor, it is aided by the iconic Singapore Girl, an enduring symbol of what the airline stands for: warm Asian hospitality that comforts passengers by creating a familiar experience on all flights. The Singapore Girl provides the brand **X-factor** that has taken decades of consistent delivery to command the steadfast loyalty of many passengers. The staff and crew at all touch points uphold this brand **eXpectation**. Gentleness, warmth, attention to detail, and a willingness to go above and beyond in the service of passengers, lends Singapore Airlines impeccable brand **eXecution** that even other airlines talk about.

7: VUELING – ACT LIKE A STARTUP

They Did It for Fun

You don't often hear about a slow work day in the airline business, but maybe that's what was happening in the IT department at Vueling, the Spanish low cost carrier, on the day the wacky idea came up. Or maybe it was just a normal, fast-moving, high-pressure work day, but the idea was so weird and fun, and the team was so fantastically geeky, that it went from being an idea, to a murmur, to a consensus, and, finally, to a plan.

We are referring, of course, to Vueling's Spring 2015 launch of its Game of Thrones internet booking engine. Thanks to a lot of ingenuity and hard work that went well beyond the airline's IT department, anyone with internet access can now book a flight to any of the Seven Kingdoms via Vueling's Game of Thrones site, whose launch was timed to coincide with the start of the fifth season of the wildly popular TV show based on the series of novels by George R. R. Martin. A banner at the top of the booking site's home page declares: "You don't have to fly to the 7 Kingdoms and cross the Narrow Sea on a dragon—Vueling will take you!" You are prompted to begin your booking by choosing what time you want to fly: dawn, twilight, or "time of the walkers," and whether you prefer to fly as a Villager, a Lord, or a King. Having made those selections, you are then moved to a screen where you enter "your" name—which you may choose from among the seven clan names from the series: Targaryen, Baratheon, et cetera. You then get to pick your seating ("Iron Throne," "Casterly Rock Throne," "I Renounce the Throne," etc.). You can add travel insurance (an escort by the Unsullied Warriors), medical insurance (a flask of antidote to poison), and special baggage (chests of gold, ivory and skins). Finally, having paid for your flight in the currency of your choice (Silver Moons, Copper Stars…), you can book a room at the Three Dragons Inn, and reserve a rental horse for local transport at your destination.

Of course, all of this is entirely fake. Vueling has not made a penny in direct revenue from this site. And although they are an excellent, highly profitable low-cost airline, they will not be able to transport you into the fictional world of Game of Thrones. So why did a real airline create a detailed fake booking website? As far as we can discern from our conversations with numerous Vueling personnel, the answer is a very strange one: they did it for fun.

The Game of Thrones idea did not, after all, come from the marketing or sales department. Creating synergy between the Vueling brand and the TV show was not the motivation either. Samuel Lacarta, director of IT at Vueling, said the idea for the site was something his department had been joking about for a while. There was already a shared affinity in the department for comic book and fantasy culture. Vueling IT people had a lot of in-jokes, like naming servers after comic book heroes. Then the Game of Thrones idea picked up enough momentum that it finally rose above the level of a joke and became, "Hey, what if we actually do this?" Sam recalls, "The team challenged me, saying, 'Now if you're brave enough, you can go present it.' I did! The Commercial Director listened to me and said, 'It sounds like fun. Don't break anything. Show it to me before you go Live.'"

Before long, the project spread beyond IT and personnel from other departments were involved. Marion Bauer, Vueling's E&M Commerce director, got her people in the game: "While the guys were programming and trying to find out how we could do it, from my side they were designing and doing copies and doing a list of specifications, so the guys could run it." People were excited and were enjoying themselves, and also working quite hard, putting in all the hours it takes to code, design, and launch a multi-page website at a multi-million-dollar company. At a certain point, Sam says, "I had to tell the team, 'Hey guys, we shouldn't be spending too much time on this. It's not real business. This is not what they're paying us for.' So it ended up being something that most of them were working on outside of business hours because they just wanted to be a part of it."

The marketing of the site had a similar grassroots vibe about it. As Sam told us, "Most of the initial social media stuff, it was just us telling our friends, 'Hey, have you seen this?'" This eventually blew up into millions of people visiting the fake booking site. Again, the site made no direct tie-in to any real-world product that Vueling offers, but it did create extended exposure to the brand for a huge number of people who hadn't ever flown the airline or necessarily even heard of it. "It was like that," Sam says. "It was crazy. It was a good one."

If you happen to be in the marketing department at a low-cost airline, at this point you are probably thinking to yourself, "How can I replicate this in my business?" The answer is that you probably can't. Sure, other airlines have associated themselves in creative and successful ways with icons of popular culture. As we've discussed in other chapters of this book, Turkish Airlines launched a wildly successful series of online ads featuring international sports stars Kobe Bryant and Lionel Messi; Finnair featured Japanese film star Koji

Yakusho in an ad campaign that increased travel between Japan and Europe, and called upon skateboarding champion Arto Saari to host an international event in which skateboarders took over Helsinki Airport. But what Vueling did is really a whole different animal, for two reasons: one, the airline's executives didn't drive it—they allowed it and facilitated it; and two, it was not strictly motivated by any kind of brand strategy, as the above-mentioned airlines' pop culture initiatives were—it was, again, just a group of rank-and-file employees at an airline having fun.

Hiring for Attitude, Not Aptitude

So the lesson here is not so much about a particular marketing initiative as it is about a company culture. For one thing, Vueling tends to hire people young. According to Alex Cruz, Vueling's CEO from 2009 to 2016, the average age of a Vueling employee is 28. We are not saying that "hire young" is a universal recipe for success. Again, looking to some of the other airlines we've discussed in this book, we see different strategies around hiring and retention: at Finnair, and Singapore Airlines, for example, age and experience are valued, and it's not unusual for employees to stay at those airlines for decades. But at Vueling youth just happens to be a central ingredient in company culture and it works for them.

Alex Cruz—who started ClickAir in 2006 and became CEO of Vueling when it absorbed ClickAir in 2009—is generally credited with building Vueling into the outstanding low-cost airline brand it has become. But he said retention was a big problem in his early days at Vueling: 50 percent of new hires didn't stay at the company for more than six months. In response to this problem, they revamped their screening process. "A significant amount of attention has to go towards understanding the personality, the values of the people, how they will manage themselves and the company when they begin to work with others…. When you are talking about people that are going to have some responsibility in a company, we do have to go through a more involved screening process that goes beyond just interviews and showing the CV. It has to go to specific tests, conversations, putting people through certain situations just to see how they would react."

When we asked Alex to give an example of a test, conversation, or situation he might use in screening a new hire, he said, "So we sit around the table and I tell them, 'I'd like you to tell me which is the worst-performing market in Vueling at the moment. And what is it that we can do about it? You have one hour.'"

At this point, he said, "Some people are lost. Some people don't move. So they just begin to write on a piece of paper. Some people get up and they ask me or they ask somebody, 'Can I go move around?' Which is the first clue. We say, 'Absolutely, you can go anywhere around the company and move around.' Now we haven't told the people in the company that they may be approached by strangers.

"The fact is, you are trying to look for people that will have initiative and that will be innovative in the way that they are going to answer the question, and when they answer the question, they are not intimidated by it. Of course, you are not looking for an exact outcome of the question, which a lot of people get distracted by. It's about capturing the moment: 'I'm being tested more for how I'm going to tackle the problem than for the solution itself.' It speaks a lot about the people that come in…. We hire much more for attitude than aptitude."

This hiring philosophy results a group of employees who create a lively office atmosphere. As Alex told the audience for his speech at the World's Low Cost Carriers Congress in 2015, "If you walk through our offices, you'll see people who you could probably place very well in some funky office in San Francisco because of the way they behave, the way they talk, what they wear, what they're looking at on the screen. Vueling is not a place that enforces heavy web-surfing policies and things like that. Frankly, we're reinforced by personally defined objectives and then, from there, you can do whatever you want to do."

An Unusual Company Culture

One of the most remarkable things Alex said to us—something we have not heard any other CEO say—was not just about his employees' attitude in general, but about their attitude toward Vueling in particular. At Vueling, he said, "There are a lot of really good individuals who are not interested in adhering themselves to a 'Go, go, go, go Vueling!' culture. They are just really good professionals. And their needs are about 'I have a job, and I will do the best job possible at my job.' It's nice to have [the 'Go, go Vueling!' attitude], but I don't really care about it so much. I need to take care of those people as well because they are an integral part of the company."

Let's just pause and think for a moment about how counter-intuitive a statement this is for a leader to make. Alex is basically saying that the way to cultivate internal brand loyalty is to value your employees who don't have strong brand loyalty, but who have their own reasons for wanting to do a good job. This is a very Zen leadership philosophy, and it has worked very well for Vueling.

And it goes further: "There are a lot of people that leave Vueling that end up in some kickass jobs because Vueling is recognized as a good brand. A lot of other companies want to have skills that people have at Vueling. And I cannot retain them." Let's be clear about something: Alex was not lamenting when he said he that can't retain his employees. He was bragging. He was bragging that his employees get poached by the very best! He was also acknowledging that as a low-cost carrier, Vueling simply does not have the budget to pay its people at the highest rates, "So they get a call from a headhunter, and they could easily be offered double that amount."

On the subject of having his employees poached, let us just add one more remarkable thing that Alex—who himself recently moved on to the higher-profile CEO role at British Airways—said about the relationship between those employees and Vueling: "And then you, as an individual, have to make a choice: 'Have I finished my career here? Is there more that I can extract to grow myself as an individual? What is important for me in my life?' I respect all the decisions people take."

In other words, the ex-Commander in Chief of Vueling is saying basically the opposite of US President John F. Kennedy's famous aphorism: "Ask not what you can do for Vueling; ask what Vueling can do for you."

Of course it's not quite that simple. You grow in a job to the extent that you push yourself to take on challenges—to try new things and to do the old things better than you'd done them previously. And if you do succeed in growing, that's unquestionably going to benefit the company. Alex recognizes that motivating employees is not just a question of convincing them to deliver an excellent product or service for the sake of the brand, but allowing them the opportunity to achieve that excellence for its own sake.

A perfect example is the Game of Thrones booking engine. At a more buttoned-up company, where what people are looking at on their computer screens is more carefully monitored, and where it is communicated to employees in a dozen different ways that their job does not include coming up with goofy, non-revenue-producing ideas, the Game of Thrones site would never have gotten past the joke stage.

There is an interesting subtext to the young, lively culture at Vueling. No one we spoke to said this in so many words, but especially given Alex's comment about headhunters offering Vueling people double the salary at another company, it's reasonable to assume that one of the primary reasons the demographics at Vueling skew so young is simply a matter of economics: the airline does not have the budget to hire senior people in the industry for every single role. But that old adage "Necessity is the mother of invention" fits this situation to a T. Economics require you to hire mostly young, inexperienced people, so what do you do? You play to their strengths. You give them free reign to set personal goals and achieve them, to have fun, to bring in off-the-grid ideas, to innovate.

A Tech Innovator

And innovate they have. The Game of Thrones site wins for imagination and sheer exuberance, but at the purely tech level it is far from being the most innovative thing Vueling has done in the last decade.

Although Vueling does not have an official policy, as Google does, of asking employees to devote a certain number of hours per month to non-task-specific experimentation, that sort of thing happens at Vueling on an ad hoc basis, when time permits. This has resulted in Vueling getting out ahead of most other low cost airlines on new products and services.

Innovation does not always originate in the IT department, either. It was someone from accounting who came up with the Fare Lock idea. How many times have you been trying to book your holiday trip, seen a great fare, called your spouse to make sure the date and time work, then called your mother-in-law who's also traveling with you, and by the time you got back to that great fare, it wasn't so great anymore? The Vueling accountant's solution was simple. When you find that great fare, you can pay just two Euros per passenger to save it for 24 hours without actually buying the tickets yet. If you get an okay from your family, you go back and buy the tickets. If not, you cancel without having to pay the full price of the ticket.

Like Game of Thrones, Fare Lock is not so much a cutting-edge tech innovation as a clever application of technology that's been around for a while. But Vueling has also repeatedly been a first adopter of freshly minted technology that hasn't yet found a use in the airline industry. Vueling was the very first airline in the world to create a booking app for a smart phone. In 2009, the airline launched apps on both iPhone and Android platforms. Since then they have been striving continually to make the smart phone app the easiest and quickest possible experience for their customers.

Google recently tested Vueling's mobile booking apps and found that if you are not logged in to the app, you can book a flight in a minute and 20 seconds, and if you are logged in, you can book in 42 seconds. Yes, you read that correctly, you can book a Vueling flight on your phone or tablet in 42 seconds. The design and implementation of Vueling's mobile booking has become so successful that two million people have downloaded it, and use it an average of one-and-a-half times a month. A full 12 percent of all Vueling's bookings come from mobile devices.

Vueling achived another first in the spring of 2015, when they were the first airline in the world to create an app for the Apple Watch. The rollout was timed to coincide with the European launch of the watch itself. The app is available in Spanish, Catalan, English, Italian, French, German, and Dutch versions. It allows passengers to view all their future Vueling reservations, and has a "Glance" feature that shows real-time data on the day of the flight, including flight number, seat, route, terminal, scheduled departure time, gate, seat, and flight status. The app will also send a message to passengers notifying them of any last-minute changes.

The Apple Watch idea came, not surprisingly, from the IT department. As Sam Lacarta said of his team, "Obviously, as techies, they will be knowledgeable of some technology from the very early stages." That was what happened with the Apple Watch. "Part of the team came and said, 'Hey, we've got this better API (application program interface). Why don't we just try it and go live first?"

Since Sam is the responsible executive in the tech division of

Vueling, he is of course thinking of the company's bottom line—"I have to say that there are a very few things that we do that we don't have investment on the scope." So he had to know that being the first airline in the world to use smart watch technology was going to be good PR for the airline—and it has been, absolutely. As Alex told us, "In short haul travel in most parts of the world, brand is irrelevant.... 80 percent of decisions are made exclusively on price.... [So] brand becomes a tool to be able to offer differentiation." On the differentiation question Alex has also said, "Ultimately, the speed at which you're able to develop these new features... is what's going to give you an edge. There isn't a sustained platform of differentiation. There just isn't. You need to be able to continue building that over time, assuming the moment you released it that someone else is going to copy it."

A lot of the ways Vueling has been able to stay ahead of the curve on differentiation have happened as a result of the speed and flexibility with which the airline has been able to bring out technological advances. Obviously Sam Lacarta is aware of how crucial his department is to Vueling's brand differentiation, but he nonetheless modestly claims, "PR is not something that comes out of my lips, it's beyond my knowledge." And he is at least as motivated by the task itself as by its outcome: "I'm an engineer. The reason you become an engineer is because you want to create and build things." He recognizes that the same is true of his team: "Obviously you have to give them some room to do the things that they are passionate about. Otherwise, if they just do what they are told to do, it is not fun." And there it is again, the F word, fun. With the smart watch app we're talking about a different order of fun than Game of Thrones-type fun. The smart watch app is the kind of innovation that uses cutting-edge technology to facilitate commercial air travel that ultimately may pave the way for global economic growth. So this is a serious kind of fun.

Business Class on a Low-Cost Carrier

In terms of brand differentiation, perhaps Vueling's most striking innovation has not been in technology, but in service. Achieving another first, in January of 2012 the airline rolled out its business class offering. Being a low-cost airline and a short-haul airline, Vueling's business class seats are not like those of, say, Finnair or Singapore Airlines, where you get a seat significantly larger than its economy class counterpart, which also folds out into a bed. Vueling uses the same actual seats for its Excellence (business class) passengers as for its Basic (economy) passengers, but gives them more leg room as the seats are in the first row. Additionally, in a row of three Excellence seats, the airline also leaves the middle seat empty, so every passenger gets more room to spread out.

The airline added a number of service amenities too. Excellence passengers get flexibility on changing or canceling a flight, a fast track through security, VIP lounge access, priority boarding, an assigned seat, a free checked bag, a hot meal, a hot towel, and a delightful amenity that is a throwback to the Golden Age of Aviation—a free newspaper.

While marketing at Vueling can sometimes bubble up in unconventional ways, the marketing of the new business class offering was carefully planned and executed. One of the most charming and creative initiatives was to have a businessman handing out leaflets to pedestrians on the streets of Barcelona. You may be thinking, "Leaflets don't sound that creative," but let us add that the man was sitting on top of a human-size cloud whose movements seemed to be controlled by his thoughts. And the leaflets looked like boarding cards. And people actually wanted to take them from the man—and of course film him with their phones. The campaign was a collaboration between Vueling and the advertising agency OMD, who came up with the idea of hiding a Segway under a 3D model of Vueling's signature cloud. While this marketing campaign did have elements of a straightforward leaflet approach, it was also infused with a "wow" factor comparable to Kulula's putting rolling beds and bathtubs in airports at holiday time, ensuring that people's curiosity would be so piqued that they would actually read the leaflets. It amounted to a miniature sales pitch.

Vueling's business class has been a huge success for the airline. They had been facing fierce competition from Europe's two biggest low-cost carriers, easyJet and Ryanair. Ryanair in particular had aggressively increased its presence at Vueling's home airport, El Prat in Barcelona, such that between 2010 and 2011 Vueling's share of passengers at El Prat fell from 25 percent to 23 percent. But by 2014, two years after the launch of its business class, Vueling was up to a whopping 37 percent passenger share. Now a full 40 percent of its customers are business passengers, as opposed to both Ryanair and easyJet, whose business passengers comprise 25 percent or less of their total.

It is uncommon for low cost airlines to offer a business class offering. Most airline executives believe that the upside of higher yielding passengers is not as much as the downside of doing away with the simplicity of a single class offering. However, Vueling is one of the few low cost airlines to have made a business class offering work successfully. They have achieved this primarily by packaging the services for premium passengers innovatively rather than investing in a new physical product.

Synergy Between Departments

Another innovation in the area of premium service that has set Vueling apart from other low-cost airlines is its offering of connecting flights. While a common practice at legacy airlines, low-cost airlines offer point-to-point tickets between two locations only. A passenger who wants to travel between two cities for which the airline does not offer direct service has to book a flight from City A to the airline's hub, and then separately book a second flight from the hub to City B. Vueling allowed its customers to reserve flights from City A to their Barcelona hub to City B all on one booking. This was another crucial turning point in the history of Vueling's brand differentiation. Like the launch of Excellence fares, the connecting flights offering was about Vueling building its identity as the low-cost carrier that offers service on a par with legacy carriers.

The connecting flights initiative required the involvement of multiple divisions of the airline. The IT department had to revamp the entire Vueling website. Sam told us it required a year's worth of work, and that the actual launch of the site took 14 hours. "It was very big team here working together, I think it was around 60 people. It was not only IT, but also many people from airports, customer care, marketing, different areas, making sure that all the processes were working. We changed the website and most of the satellite systems and that had been very well-prepared. We started on a Saturday around 7 p.m. And we started preparing some of the things. We brought the website down and it was up sometime early in the morning. And we continued the testing. I remember it was midday on Sunday when we finished. Everyone was really exhausted. We were not even able to celebrate because we were so tired. When you put a rocket on the moon, it was a similar feeling."

The synergy between departments is part of what makes Vueling function so well as a company. The connecting flights initiative came from the top down, but the culture at Vueling is such that who comes up with the idea or gives the directive matters less than the spirit of working together and sharing a sense of purpose.

In our experience working with a lot of other airlines, that is not always the case. Our team at SimpliFlying had a meeting with the marketing department of an airline not long ago where we made some recommendations. The response was, "We all want to do all these things that you are suggesting. But how can we skip IT?

How can we not talk to IT?" When we asked them why, they said, "Because IT will tell us to come back six months later, as they have other priorities right now."

We asked Sam how he manages to run an IT department that doesn't inspire that kind of reluctance in other departments. He said, "We need to be fast enough to keep up with the business needs and also to avoid what I would call 'shadow IT,' which is IT that does not happen in the company's own IT department, or when there's a provider that goes to the marketing department and says, 'We can build this platform and this is the turnkey solution. You don't need any integration, you don't need your own IT department.'"

At Vueling, there is less of a clear boundary between one department and the next than at most airlines, less of a distinction between one person's job duties and another's. Marion Bauer confessed to us that "I'm in the sales department but my desk is not in the sales area, it's in the IT area because I asked for it." There's crossover at every level. Pilots now receive training in social media to keep them abreast of changing passenger behaviors. Alex himself famously lends a hand in surprising ways. At Bilbao Airport not long ago, the CEO was a passenger on an aircraft that had a flat tire. He went up to the cockpit and spoke to the pilot. "I saw that he was very busy, so I said, 'Do you want me to talk to your passengers?' He said, 'Yeah, why not? You will save me some time.' So Alex got on the plane's PA and announced in Spanish that there was a flat tire, there would be a 45-minute delay, and the flight attendants would be coming around with water for everyone. Then he made the announcement in English. Someone on the plane immediately tweeted this, accompanied by a photo of Alex making the announcement, and so a little PR bump for Vueling was inadvertently born.

Alex didn't think much of it at the time, but he said his attitude is as important or more important than everyone else's. "I mean I'm the guy that turns off the lights, I am the last one that leaves here....

If you are part of a team and you are inside of an airplane and you see they are busy, you offer to help. It's what makes sense." That is the kind of sense of responsibility, starting from the top of the organizational chart, that permeates the company culture.

Responding to Customers' Needs

The customers, of course, also receive the benefits of such a well-integrated culture. And customer care is another important way that Vueling has been able to compete successfully with other European low-cost carriers. When you've got people working successfully together, they are likely to be able to listen well to customer feedback and respond accordingly. A case in point was back in the summer and fall of 2012. In August of that year, a Vueling flight going from Malaga, Spain, to Amsterdam had a miscommunication with air traffic control at Amsterdam's Schiphol Airport, resulting in the mistaken idea that the flight was being hijacked. Dutch F-16 fighter jets were scrambled to accompany the flight, and before the mistake was resolved, false news of the hijacking had spread like wildfire on social media.

More than one tweet per second started appearing on Twitter in response to the hijacking that wasn't. Vueling was slow to respond. This is somewhat understandable, because they did not want to release any information before they had complete knowledge of what was going on. But as Simpliflying's consultant Marco Serusi pointed out at the time, the airline told mainstream news outlets that the hijacking was a false alarm nearly half an hour before they got around to announcing it on Twitter to calm the furor there. They also failed to use the hashtags #hijacking and #Amsterdam that had accompanied many of the related tweets, thereby diminishing the chances of reaching all the people who'd been getting false information about the hijacking. Finally, they tweeted the accurate information only in Spanish, despite many of the false tweets about the hijacking having been written in English and Dutch.

You might be thinking that a half an hour is a paltry amount of time. But consider that at a rate of more than one tweet per second, with an average of 126 followers per user, a 30-minute delay gives the false news a reach of 226,800 users. That's a lot of people associating an airline with a terrifying event.

This was an anomaly for Vueling, which has been quite consistently astute in its use of social media. And the good news is they learned quickly from their mistake. In September, a bird strike caused a Vueling aircraft to land prematurely in Barcelona to perform mandatory safety checks. The tweet storm ensued almost immediately, with incomplete information. But this time the Vueling social media team stayed on top of the situation. Despite the fact that the bulk of the tweets happened on a Saturday and a Sunday, Vueling sent more than 330 replies to users who'd tweeted about the issue, even when their tweets were not addressed directly to the airline. Vueling also reached out via Twitter to the mainstream media and to influential bloggers who'd been posting about the plane's unexpected landing, and they did so in multiple languages.

Every company makes mistakes, and this pair of incidents speaks well of the airline's capacity to learn from theirs. In the course of less than a month Vueling proved itself to be very responsive to the needs of its public. Not surprising for an airline that values and celebrates acts of generosity and selflessness in others.

Stories that Deserve a Plane

The celebration we are specifically referring to is an initiative the airline started in 2015 when they were renewing their fleet. They decided to honor people around the world who had acted in quietly heroic ways by putting their names on an aircraft. They started a website, storiesthatdeserveaplane.org, where people could nominate unknown heroes whose names they thought should be printed on the side of a Vueling plane. Vueling chose a couple named Arelis and Carlos Vasquez, who own a dry cleaning business in New York City. In 2008, when the stock market crashed and a lot of people lost their jobs, Arelis and Carlos hung a sign in the window of their shop saying "If you are unemployed and need an outfit cleaned for an interview, we will clean it for free." As of this writing, long after the US economy has bounced back, the sign still hangs in the Vasquez' shop window, and their names now grace the side of a plane in the Vueling fleet. Same is true of Miguel Angel Galán, who owns a football academy in Getafe, Spain. When Miguel saw the now-infamous photo of a Hungarian journalist tripping a Syrian refugee who was carrying his son, he decided to offer the Syrian dad a job at his school. Osama Abdul Mohsen now works for Miguel at Getafe Coach Training Center, and Osama's wife and children live with him in Getafe.

This is a marketing campaign with a heart and a soul, not surprising for an airline that prides itself on putting people first.

A New CEO Makes a Bold Move

In April of 2016 Alex Cruz moved on to the CEO position at British Airways, and Javier Sánchez-Prieto, who had been CFO of Iberia, moved into the top spot at Vueling. In less than six months, he had introduced a new initiative that took the airline's differentiation to a new level. As of September 2016, Vueling codeshares with Qatar Airways. Now Vueling carries Qatar Airways' QR code on 67 of its European routes. This includes 49 of its flights out of Barcelona and 19 out of Rome, covering a total of 52 unique destinations. Of those 52 destinations, 48 will be new to Qatar customers.

Codesharing is not unusual in the airline business, but what is unusual is a full-service airline like Qatar partnering with a low-cost airline like Vueling. The big obstacle to such arrangements is typically the difference in service quality between the two airlines, and their IT systems. But because Vueling has already distinguished itself with premium service offerings, the differences in service will be far less noticeable. Qatar customers on flights codeshared by Vueling will have access to Vueling's Excellence seating and other Excellence amenities, and will be able to earn Qmiles on their Vueling flights. Thus the new CEO continues to create a distinctive brand identity for the airline.

6X Analysis

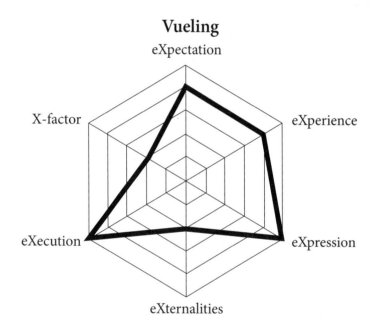

Vueling

Standout features of Vueling on the 6X scale are **eXpression** and **eXecution**, followed closely by **eXpectation** and **eXperience**.

The brand is particularly strong on how it **eXpresses** its values to its own employees. In a beautiful paradox, it expresses them by not expressing them too much. It empowers employees by letting them know that the big ideas can come from them, based on personal standards they have set for their own performance. The young, start-up-style culture at Vueling strongly rewards innovation, whether it be of the purely fun variety like the Game of Thrones booking site, or of the revenue-building, brand-building, industry-leading variety, like the smart phone and smart watch apps, both launched before any other airline had engaged those technologies. Customer **eXperience** also benefits by the strong tech culture at Vueling. The mobile app is streamlined and easy to use (remember the astonishing 42 seconds it takes to book a Vueling flight on a mobile device) without sacrificing the full range of Vueling products, from the three different fare options—Basic, Optima, and Excellence—to the availability of connecting flights. With its high profile as an innovator and its niche as the low cost airline that delivers an unusually high quality of service, Vueling is successful in the **eXpectation** arena as well.

Leadership is surely a big strength in the **eXecution** category. Beginning when he took over as CEO in 2009, the charismatic Alex Cruz built the brand into what it is today. Employee empowerment and internal brand resonance are also great strengths of brand **eXecution**. New CEO Javier Sánchez-Prieto takes the reins at an exciting moment, as Vueling is set to expand its fleet to more than 100 aircraft. Vueling's growth in the last half-decade has been phenomenal, and Javier's challenge will be to keep the culture fresh, agile, and innovative as the company's global footprint continues to grow.

8: AIR NEW ZEALAND: A LITTLE AIRLINE FROM THE CORNER OF THE WORLD, NO MORE

From a Nation's Beginning to an Airline's Rebirth

Every nation has an origin myth, and the star of New Zealand's origin myth is a man named Kupe. According to the mythology of the indigenous Maori people, Kupe, a Tahitian chief, was the first Polynesian to set foot in New Zealand. The story goes like this: Sometime around the 10th century in Tahiti, Kupe and his people were facing grave difficulties. His rival, Muturangi, was allowing his pet giant octopus to swim near the fishing nets of Kupe's people, scaring away all the fish. Even after repeated entreaties from Kupe, Muturangi refused to call off the giant octopus, so Kupe decided he had to kill the monster. He set out toward the octopus in a canoe, but the octopus was very fast, and kept swimming away from him. The octopus drew Kupe thousands of miles out to sea, until they came to the two islands that comprise New Zealand, where Kupe finally slew the beast. He was so taken with the new islands that he went back home and returned with his family.

Fast forward a thousand years. Like Kupe, Air New Zealand was facing grave difficulties. In 2000 the airline acquired Ansett, a struggling Australian airline, from Rupert Murdoch's News Corporation. Over time, with key shareholder support to renew the airline withdrawn, Ansett proceeded to lose more than a million dollars a day. In Easter of 2001 when Ansett was expecting its strongest revenue day ever, its aging fleet of Boeing 767s was temporarily grounded by Australian regulators (who eventually found no defects). By the end of September, within weeks of the 9/11 attacks in the United States, Air New Zealand posted a stunning loss of $1.425 billion, the largest in New Zealand's corporate history at that time. To put it in mythological terms, a giant octopus was scaring all the fish away from Air New Zealand's nets.

Enter Ralph Norris, the first of a series of three CEOs who have slain the octopus and saved the airline. One of the first things Norris did when he took over in 2002 was to conduct a staff survey. The results were alarming. Only 29 percent of employees even bothered to respond. Of that 29 percent, 90 percent expressed no confidence in the airline's management or their plans for the future. With limited resources, aging equipment, and disgruntled people, Ralph Norris did something remarkable: He chose to focus on the people—both the customer-facing staff and passengers themselves. He decided that customer service was the most important area to revive and put the company back on its feet. He instituted a 30 percent pay cut for the management, eliminated perks like chauffeur-driven limousines, and eventually let go of 40 senior managers. The emphasis on company culture has carried through the two CEOs who have followed Norris, Rob Fyfe and the airline's current chief, Christopher Luxon. Everyone we interviewed, from managers to customer service agents, talked about wanting to invest their time, energy, and passion in the company because the company invests in them.

Once the people part of the equation was taken care of, attention was then turned to the fleet. The airline refurbished its 747 fleet and introduced some new 777-200s. But the big move came with the purchase of a fleet of new 777-300s. This was part of a plan to make Air New Zealand a strong contender in the long-haul travel market. Not coincidentally, the long-haul initiative was named the Kupe Project, in honor of the Tahitian chief who improbably traveled halfway across the Pacific Ocean to New Zealand in a canoe. The airline began introducing new long haul-flights, and increased its footprint in Asia, Europe, and North America. Since it was a fairly small airline without a sizable local customer base, competing against the established giants in the field, the team recognized they would have to do more than roll out a new fleet. They would have to come up with something new and fresh to distinguish themselves, something that no one else had.

"Why Didn't You People Think of That?"

They began with what was already becoming their sweet spot, the customer experience. The obvious place to look to improve customer experience would have been business class. But, as we were told by Kerry Reeves, Head of Aircraft Programs, "We were given a mandate of reinventing travel—not in business class, because anybody can do that, but in economy and premium economy." They did workshops, they did focus groups, and the most powerful thing they did was just to watch people fly. Kerry and his team spent a lot of time on Air New Zealand flights observing passengers, and particularly homing in on what made them uncomfortable. Their customers' pain points would spur their innovation.

The team noticed that passengers on long-haul flights that were not at full capacity would immediately stake their claim on an empty row so they could lie down, and "hope that it wasn't a designer seat where the armrests torture you by only going halfway up." Kerry and the team also noticed that young children inhabit airplanes differently than adults, in that they try to lie down on the on the flat surface of the floor in the area below the seats, however this is against the safety requirements.

So the team brought in IDEO, a U.S. design firm famous for designing Apple's first mouse, to help understand the user perspective. From this the team began to look at a seat re-design that would allow passengers in economy to make a choice between lying down and sitting up, whenever they wished, and might also give little kids a more suitable surface to play on. They came up with Economy Skycouch™. The Skycouch is three economy seats that convert to a couch when you pull back the armrests, and then convert to a flat flexible space when you flip up the leg rests. Passengers who have booked a Skycouch also get a mattress and large pillows to use during the flight.

This turns out to be one of those inventions that has people wondering why it hadn't been invented sooner. In fact, Kerry Reeves told us that Sir Tim Clark, CEO of Emirates Airline, saw Skycouch at an aviation product show, turned to his team, and said, "That's just a seat with a leg rest that comes all the way up. Why didn't you people think of that?"

Passengers took to it as well. They used it in the ways the Kupe team had intended: They slept on it; and when it was deployed flat, kids played on its surface while parents could ease up on the constant vigilance and awkward, cramped positions ordinarily required of them on long-haul flights. But then a funny thing happened. People began finding uses for it that the team who designed it had not anticipated. Couples began booking Skycouch and spooning on it during sleeping hours, motivating the airline to market it as "the cuddle couch." And then there were individual passengers who wanted the comfort of a business-class seat but had no interest in the more luxurious level of service in business class, so they, too, started booking Skycouch, which cost them about 80 percent of what a business seat would have. So it is one of those innovations that has proven to have uses far more versatile than even its designers envisioned.

The airline took a patent out on the seat design, and has now licensed it to three other airlines—none of them direct competitors. So the Skycouch, you might say, has legs. Kerry Reeves says there are two basic kinds of innovations. There are those innovations that are so technical that no one understands them. The return of investment on such innovations is strictly about how they affect the company's bottom line. If they make or save the company money, then they were worth the expense of inventing and implementing. The other kind of innovation is one that is publicly demonstrable and understood. The return on investment of this second kind of innovation extends beyond its direct effect on the company's bottom line. Skycouch falls squarely in the second category of innovation. As Kerry put it, "The intangible value is that it's talked about, the fact that in New Zealand, we developed the Skycouch. So it's not just what it's done for our passengers. It's what it's also done for our company and promoting New Zealand."

Safety Has Never Been So Enjoyable

As we said, the magic of the Skycouch was that once it was invented, everyone wondered why it hadn't been invented sooner. But Skycouch is not Air New Zealand's only innovation that possesses that kind of magic. There are also the world-famous safety videos. Sure, other airlines had created safety videos with high production values for the longest time, but it had never occurred to any of them to make a safety video that was actually entertaining and fun and could be used as marketing collateral.

As with many innovations of lasting value, Air New Zealand's funny safety videos started as a way of overcoming a problem. The problem was that Air New Zealand was a legacy airline competing with low-cost upstarts in a market that had already experienced a downturn. The airline set out to show would-be customers that although its price point was higher than that of low-cost carriers

(LCCs), its fares contained no hidden fees, as the LCCs' fares often did. So in 2009 it created a video called "Nothing to Hide," in which actual airline staff were filmed wearing nothing but body paint that was made to look like the Air New Zealand uniform. An airport service agent, baggage handlers, and a flight attendant were shown doing their jobs in the buff while passengers looked on with eyes and mouths wide open. Then CEO Rob Fyfe even made a cameo as a baggage handler. The video went viral on the internet.

Taking the cue from the advertisement, Air New Zealand soon launched a safety video titled "Bare Essentials of Safety," featuring— you guessed it—naked flight attendants in body paint. As *New York Times* business writer Bettina Wassener put it, "Passengers… may have never paid more rapt attention to the line 'undo the seat belt by lifting the metal flap.'" And not only passengers. The video went viral so fast that it briefly crashed Air New Zealand's website. Amazingly, it took only a day to shoot from beginning to end and it cost the airline about 10 to 15 percent of a typical commercial for a major brand, mainly because they didn't have to pay actors and fly them in. As the *Times'* Wassener cheekily put it, "The Air New Zealand staff members did not receive extra pay, just increased exposure."

As with Skycouch, the "Bare Essentials" video represented a radical change in commercial aviation that no one knew they wanted until they had it. Virgin Atlantic and Delta Air Lines and others have followed suit with their own fun safety videos but Air New Zealand got there first. "Bare Essentials" created a big boost for airline safety, for the airline, and for New Zealand as a whole. At the time it hit the internet, it was the most-watched video clip ever to come out of New Zealand. The video has over 7.5 million views on YouTube to date.

So fine, a one-off, a fluke, impossible to repeat, because as everyone knows, you can't create a viral video, you can only create a video and hope it goes viral. Except that Air New Zealand did it again. And again.

Departing from the low-budget, celebrity-free approach of the "Bare Essentials" video, the airline amped it up with the irrepressible TV fitness personality Richard Simmons, who led a safety workout in a video called "Fit to Fly." With a fitness-disco beat in the background, Simmons—sporting a spangly tank top emblazoned with Air New Zealand's *koru* logo—gleefully exhorts passengers to "stretch it out and *lose that baggage!* Stretch it up to the overhead locker, or slide it under the seat in front of you. Stretch... and slide... yeah! You're a giraffe!"

Playing on the title "Bare Essentials of Safety," the airline also made a "Bear Essentials of Safety" filmed in the wild with celebrity British wilderness adventurer Bear Grylls. The airline then did yet another with the All Blacks, New Zealand's national rugby team, to celebrate its support of them.

The airline's most watched safety video has been the aptly titled "The Most Epic Safety Video Ever Made," a Hobbit-themed video featuring cameos by the star of *The Hobbit*, Elijah Wood, and its director, Peter Jackson—a New Zealand native. Air New Zealand became "The official airline of Middle-Earth," even painting two Boeing 777s in Hobbit-inspired liveries. The airline has loaded a playlist of all its safety videos on its in-flight entertainment consoles and it is not surprising for passengers to be watching one after another before landing. That's a sight one wouldn't encounter on other airlines.

Not only has the airline hired celebrities to perform in its videos, it has also created its very own celebrity. It created a series of non-safety-related viral videos starring a puppet called Rico. A furry, talking animal of indeterminate species—part bear, part raccoon, part dingo, maybe?—Rico was Air New Zealand's spokescreature for several years running. As Head of Global Brand Jodi Williams told us, "We were after a unique and creative way of showcasing our new long-haul product and the launch of the new Economy

Skycouch and Premium Economy Spaceseat, with a focus on the North American and UK/EU markets." The roomy Spaceseat is a seating innovation the airline rolled out along with Skycouch. The Spaceseat allows a premium economy flier to recline their seat by sliding it down and forward, so that it doesn't impinge on the personal space of the passenger sitting behind them.

Air New Zealand and the agency it worked with decided on "a 'spokesperson' who could have fun, stand out, be a little cheeky, and in an engaging way showcase the benefits and features of the new products." It ended up going with an animal instead of a human because, as former CEO Rob Fyfe said, "If you put a human into the ads, you stereotype people's image of what sort of people you're trying to engage with."

Fun, cheeky, and engaging Rico certainly is. In his first appearance, he is shown reclining in a Spaceseat, conversing with a fellow (human) passenger about all the things he loved about his trip to New Zealand. A typical example is what he calls "a nice Kiwi beach." But with his European-ish accent of uncertain origin, Rico pronounces the word "beach" so that it sounds like another word referring to a female dog. This is, shall we say, one of Rico's milder affronts to polite conversation.

Some viewers were offended by Rico's racy double-entendres and irreverent attitude, but he had many fans too. The Air New Zealand marketing team was well aware that it needed to push the envelope to create awareness of the brand overseas. We are struck once again by the insight that what works for one brand would likely be a disaster for another. Can you imagine if Singapore Airlines suddenly replaced the Singapore Girl with Rico in their ads? At best, their customers would be extremely puzzled, and very likely they would be shocked. But as the feisty upstart brand with a loose and relaxed Kiwi temperament, Air New Zealand has more room to push the boundaries in its videos with nudity, humor, and a furry animal with loose morals.

That said, the execution of the Rico character and his story was hardly loose and relaxed. Quality control was meticulous. Jodi Williams said, "Size and scale were important, thinking about the environment. Quality of the physical puppet was also incredibly important, as was the voice and puppeteer. We worked with the Jim Henson company, creators of the Muppets, which designed and built the Rico and selected the puppeteer."

Rico interacted with more unnamed travelers, but as his own fame skyrocketed, he started gravitating toward other celebrities. A talk show–style segment called "On the Skycouch with Rico" was launched. In his Skycouch interview with David Hasselhoff, Rico repeatedly refers to Hasselhoff's character on the hit TV show *Baywatch* as "a mouthguard," while Hasselhoff vainly tries to tell him that he played a lifeguard. In his interview with Lindsay Lohan (shot in "Lust Angeles," of course), he tries to get Lohan to arrange "a bite of the fangs and a roll in the fur" with her friend Kim Kardashian. He even recorded a rap video with Snoop Dogg. In the end, after Rico had had a good run promoting the airline and offending people of upright sensibility, Air New Zealand decided to retire the character. But rather than let Rico fade away, they decided he should go out with a bang, killing the character off. In a promotional tie-in with the Hasbro game Cluedo, the airline created an interactive investigation in which viewers were invited to help figure out who was behind the demise of the furry creature with the potty mouth. In the end, under questioning by the actor who had played Rico, Richard Simmons confessed to the murder. His motive: envy. It turns out Rico had been able to do 25,002 jumping jacks while Simmons could only do 25,000.

Employee Empowerment

Air New Zealand's feisty, sassy marketing style resonates well with the brand's personality, but ultimately their marketing succeeds because it's backed up by an excellent product. Furthermore, as we heard repeatedly from our interviewees at the airline, the product succeeds because management believes people solve problems more effectively when they are trusted, treated with respect, and inspired by creative freedom.

Kerry Reeves, who's been with Air New Zealand since 1975, has seen a dramatic shift in company culture during his tenure. Speaking of the company before the new millennium, he said, "I've seen different areas of not so much company error, but economic errors where money was king. Culture and empathy and all that stuff weren't even talked about. So it was all about cost-cutting and all that." Innovation Manager Dave McRobie, who's been with the airline for 20 years, concurs: "When I started, this was a corporate airline. It had a very untouchable executive layer."

But in the 21st century a string of enlightened CEOs—Norris, Fyfe, and Luxon—have made a major investment in the culture. As Dave said, "You became intensely proud of where you were working. And you became very aware of how the fortunes of Air New Zealand were intertwined with the fortunes of New Zealand. So there's no doubt. Once you have that understanding fairly and squarely in your mind—and it's not marketing bulls***, it's an understanding that makes sense—all of a sudden it makes it very easy to do your job, and in my case, to do creative work."

Current CEO Christopher Luxon describes the synergy between the airline and its home country this way: "For me, the biggest thing, without a doubt, is getting connected to a mission and a purpose. You don't just do the job because you love the work in terms of the task that you have to do each day. I wake up in the morning thinking, from the time that I am at Air New Zealand, how do I want it to be when I leave? I get to steward this great company for a period of time and then I hand it over to somebody else.... I think for me personally, I get very connected in this job to the mission and purpose of how we help New Zealand economically, socially, and environmentally. That's not just motherhood. That's not just words and a vision statement. It's actually really what this company came to do each day."

That mission comes with inherent challenges. How does Air New Zealand put itself on the map as a global competitor in the long-haul market, and make its home country—a pair of relatively small islands near the bottom of the earth—a destination widely sought after by people in North America, Europe, and Asia? Christopher hears it all the time from non–New Zealanders in the aviation business who are amazed by what he has had to overcome: "Lots of people, when I go around to global aviation meetings, say to me, 'Chris, actually in New Zealand, you shouldn't exist. You are too small in an industry that's consolidating. You are on the wrong part of the world. You don't have half a billion or a couple of billion people in your catchment zone. You are all about these low-paying leisure travelers. You don't have the big corporate guys at the front end of aircraft paying exorbitant amounts of money for high business class fees….' Our competitors look at Air New Zealand and say, 'Gee, you don't have any source of competitive advantage.'"

Air New Zealand's response has been to say, *well, if we don't have a source of competitive advantage, then we'll have to make one.* That's what the Skycouch and the viral videos have been all about: creating a competitive advantage where previously there was none.

Innovation, company culture, and patriotism: These are the three strands Air New Zealand braids together to create economic success. Each is inseparable from the other two. If a company supports its employees, and demonstrates to them that their contributions not only help the company, but also help the country, that spurs more and better innovation.

Kerry Reeves said, "What was important in the Kupe Project was the trust, and the freedom that was allowed for the project team to get on and do it…. So that's very important… giving people the freedom, but not giving them the fear that they must not fail…. If you have that, then people will be much, much more creative and prepared to try something." The seating programs, Skycouch and Spaceseat, exemplify this. Not only did the team have to put a considerable amount of time and money into designing a product that passengers would love, they also had to be aware that if the seats did not pass the stringent tests for regulatory certification, they would never make it onto the planes. "You've got to be open and honest. But I expressed my confidence that I could get through this. The consequence of failure was quite high. But the management team said, 'Okay, we'll back you. If you think you can do it, then we trust you.' The decision could have been, 'We are not going to take the risk,' so therefore, we would have failed to improve that customer experience, and we might have incurred more costs, et cetera. Or we would have continued on and our team could have failed to deliver, and then the consequence would have been the aircraft are months and months late, and so on and so on."

The confidence that management showed the creative team boosted their own confidence, which spurred innovation, which enhanced both Air New Zealand's bottom line and its international reputation, which in turn benefitted the country as a whole. That is the formula that has driven and continues to drive the company's success.

The same formula is evident at the customer-service level, too. Mele Sulunga is a domestic service delivery leader in Auckland who has been promoted multiple times in her nine years with the company. She began as a customer service assistant, then she became a gate agent. As a gate agent she was asked to participate in the High Performance Engagement Project for service control, in which the company and the labor union work together to solve problems employees may be experiencing—another way in which the airline has demonstrated its commitment to the happiness of its staff. Then she was nominated to participate in the Emerging Leaders program, in which she was trained for a leadership role. After that she became a backup team manager, and from there she moved to her current position as service delivery leader. Mele confesses that until she was tapped for the Emerging Leader program, "I didn't know what direction I was taking. I didn't know my career path until I was approached by a passenger manager last year who said, 'Would you like to take this opportunity to be a part of this project?' And when I set foot on that project, I knew which career path I was going down. And from there, I stepped up and I owned it." Now she has her sights set on being an operations manager. This is all thanks to management's seeing potential in Mele and helping her to recognize that potential in herself. Underlying this approach to management is the insight that a company's growth is inextricable from the growth of its employees. "They invest so much time and money in their staff, and I'm willing to give to Air New Zealand. That's why I'm very passionate about this company."

Mele demonstrated the kind of leadership her managers recognized in her recently when bad weather in Auckland grounded all flights one night. More than a thousand passengers were affected by the delay. Mele and her staff handled a lot of disgruntled customers that night. "The majority of them were standing in the queue, of course, fuming. But when they get to a staff member... you've got to take it in because they're venting and they need you to listen, they want you to care. That's what we do. And it just takes the pressure off them."

She and her staff not only listened, but they also handled complicated logistics for all those passengers, particularly if they were from out of town. This included getting them accommodation, transporting them there, feeding them at the airline's expense, transporting them back to the airport in the morning, and getting them on the earliest possible flight. Mele and her team worked for past the end of their shift to get everyone sorted. Once they did, Mele called for an optional de-briefing session with pizza to let the staff know that they, too, were being taken care of. When we asked Mele if she got the company to reimburse her for the pizza, she was incredulous. "No. What for? This is me giving to the company." The result? Everyone stayed for the de-brief. "No one wanted to go home until everyone was ready to go home together."

Technology as Fairy Dust

The kinds of one-on-one, face-to-face interactions Mele and her team have every day are invaluable. And not surprisingly, Air New Zealand has found a way to leverage that same focus on pleasing customers across digital channels too. The Air New Zealand Fairy—who in real life is the airline's social media team—dispenses travel-related wishes and awards frequent flier points via her various social media platforms including Facebook and Twitter. Anyone can tweet to the Fairy with their wish, and it may just come true. The Fairy recently granted access to Air New Zealand's lounge to an economy passenger who was running her first New York City Marathon. One Valentine's Day, she delivered bouquets to 10 lucky customers around New Zealand. She also helps market both New Zealand and Air New Zealand by extolling the charms of the airline's destinations online.

At its annual developer conference several years ago, Google honored the Fairy by showcasing her excellent use of technology. A Google representative commented, "Air New Zealand's Fairy site is one of the most creative and innovative sites we've seen, using a range of the latest Google technologies and platforms."

Whether digital or face to face, the amount of attention Air New Zealand pays to its passengers and their needs is remarkable even in an industry that places a premium on customer satisfaction. As

Christopher said, "Every great innovation comes from customer insight." And it is a priority of the company to gather as many customer insights as it can. "We talk to 4,000 customers every month. We actually have mystery shoppers onboard. We get anecdotal evidence from customers writing to us about the good, the bad, and the ugly of their experience at Air New Zealand. So we monitor that and we review that formally every month in what we call our customer experience meeting."

The airline pays particular attention to things that cause their customers discomfort. One such discomfort arises when children are traveling unaccompanied, and their parents, grandparents, and other concerned caregivers have limited information about their youngsters' whereabouts for the duration of their trip. In response to this customer pain point, Air New Zealand developed Airband™, a small watch-like device that straps onto a child's wrist and uses near field communication (NFC) technology to trigger a notification when the airline staff scan it. Now, texts are sent to as many as five people designated to receive them when the children check in, when they are boarding the plane, when the cabin crew hands them off to ground staff after the plane has landed, and when they are picked up by the designated caregiver. These notifications give parents greater peace of mind.

Air New Zealand did not invent the underlying technology. Mobile phones and access-control cards employ NFC technology for a variety of different uses today. And Disney was the first company to use a device along the lines of Airband in order to manage the crowds at its amusement parks. Just as some customers ended up using the Skycouch differently than its originally intended purpose, so Air New Zealand's genius in this case was seeing an unanticipated use for NFC technology, adapting the technology, and applying it to an airline-specific issue.

Christopher is a big believer in looking beyond the airline

industry for ideas and solutions for airline-related problems. So he'll look not only to Disney, but also to Zappos, Four Seasons, or Netflix. Reed Hastings of Netflix is a role model for Christopher insofar as he was repeatedly willing to tear down his own business and re-build it to stay competitive. "The business was a DVD mail business and it became a streaming business and now it has become a content business."

The result is that Air New Zealand is always looking to disrupt its own way of doing things. Back in 2008, the airline was among the first to do a test flight with jatropha biofuel. The flight provided data that helped secure certification of plant-based biofuels for commercial flights. The airline's research into reducing its carbon footprint is ongoing. And what's good for the environment is good for the customers, and vice versa.

Chief Marketing and Customer Officer Mike Tod spoke to us enthusiastically about possible airline applications of the Internet of Things, in which tailoring service to a customer's individual habits and needs is inseparable from reducing the airline's environmental impact: "Imagine getting on a plane and the wine bottle talks to the wine glass, which talks to the onboard computer, which then feeds into your profile. And you get on the Air New Zealand flight tomorrow to leave this country and the flight attendant knows before you even got on the plane that on average, when you travel, you prefer to start with orange juice and that you only drink half of that orange juice, not the whole orange juice. So you get on the plane and there will be half a glass of orange juice because we are serious about not wanting to have wastage. So that helps us thinking through 300 people on a plane. If we knew that 300 people only drink half a glass of orange juice each, we'll then carry half a glass of orange juice [per person], which means we are burning a little bit less fuel."

Air New Zealand continues to innovate and to prove that a feisty little airline from a far corner of the earth can successfully compete in the long-haul market. The insight that Ralph Norris arrived at as he set out to revive the company's fortunes at the beginning of the millennium continues to drive the company today. Taking care of the needs of customers and employees will drive innovation and profit, not the other way around. Or, as Christopher puts it, "Emotional intelligence skills trump intellectual intelligence skills each and every day." Air New Zealand is a perfect example of a brand that has turned a constraint—its location—into a strength by innovating and caring about its own people. Continuing down this path should serve the brand well in an increasingly competitive industry.

6X Analysis

The areas where Air New Zealand particularly excels are **eXpectation**, **eXperience**, and **eXpression**.

The safety videos are great examples of **expectation**. The first video, "Bare Essentials of Safety," featured actual Air New Zealand staff, scoring high marks in the **authenticity** category. Its playfulness and irreverent humor showcased qualities of the Kiwi national identity that were instantly recognizable to New Zealanders, and created a positive image of New Zealand to foreigners who may not have been familiar with the country. So the videos get a big checkmark in the **resonance** column as well.

The Skycouch and Spaceseat lead the way in the **eXperience** category. The fact that these innovations brought a touch of luxury to economy and premium-economy passengers **resonates** strongly with the brand's identity. They are also products that simply deliver on their **promise** of comfort.

Air New Zealand wins a lot of points in the **eXpression** category too. The Fairy creates a fun, positive, easy **medium** for passengers to communicate their wishes and needs to the airline. Given the minute attention the airline pays to its customers' experience, and the thousands of customer surveys it collects every month, it do very well in the **feedback loop** element as well. And whether it's Mele in customer service, Kerry in aircraft programs, or Dave in innovation, staff are encouraged by management to take initiative and rely on their own skill and experience to solve problems for customers, making Air New Zealand the very embodiment of employee **empowerment**.

Note: To see what it is to fly on the Air New Zealand Boeing 787 and experience the SkyCouch, drop me a line at flyairnz@simpliflying.com and I'll send you a secret URL!

APPENDIX:
THE 6X AIRLINE
BRAND MODEL

As mentioned in the introduction of this book, airline marketing is different. Compared to any other business-to-consumer (B2C) industry, airlines require a different mindset to build their brand. The industry has its own set of complexities and opportunities, which require a bespoke approach to creating a bond with customers. The 6X airline brand model provides a framework to help airline marketers do just that, as validated by the airlines featured in *SOAR*.

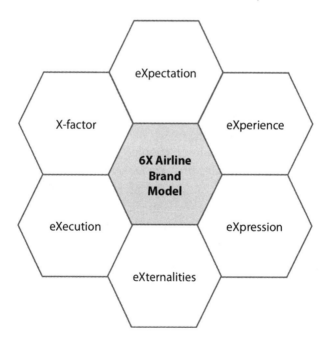

Brand eXpectation: Making an Authentic Promise

Making an authentic brand promise is the key to having satisfied customers. A strong brand promise emphasizes the airline's core identity, visual and otherwise, and reflects its clear differentiation and positioning in the marketplace. Sometimes, airlines get so consumed by day-to-day operations that they disregard this aspect of the business and end up setting false or ambiguous expectations. In other cases, brands set extremely high expectations and then fail to deliver. An accurate projection of what an airline is about and the experience it will deliver to the customer is the essence of brand *eXpectation.*

Clarity and focus should drive a brand's promise, with the aim to create a lasting impression in the potential customer's mind. Ideally, the positioning should hit logical and emotional chords and differentiate the airline from its competitors. Differentiation could come in terms of key strengths like pricing, service, or even destinations. When it comes to price differentiation, budget airlines like kulula and Southwest are some of the best. Legacy carriers like Singapore Airlines and Air New Zealand rule the skies in terms of setting expectations of exceptional service. The likes of Turkish Airlines often tout the number of destinations they fly to.

Setting the right brand expectations goes beyond the traditional advertising mediums. Efforts should be focused on reaching potential customers where they are present. Finnair and Air New Zealand are active on Chinese social networks like WeChat to reach the consumers there. The aim should be to set the right tone for the engagement. To entice the customer for the first time and subsequently induce loyalty. However, the real test of character takes place when the customer experiences the product—when he or she finally flies with the airline.

Brand eXperience: Keeping the Word

Achieved by aligning all product, service, and corporate operations to deliver the promises made while setting brand expectations, *eXperience* is probably the most important aspect of an airline's brand. The aim of providing a superlative brand experience should be to build customer loyalty. What can the airline do to make sure that customers fly with them again? Simply meet or exceed expectations.

Brand *eXperience* is fostered across multiple touchpoints, from the booking hotline and website, to the check-in row and on board the plane. This also provides multiple opportunities to bring forth the brand personality of the airline. Something unique to airlines is the length of the customers' experience with the brand. For the duration of the flight, as well as before and after, airlines owe it to themselves to leave an indelible impression on the customer that keeps them coming back for more. Often, airlines spend a lot of attention on frequent fliers, but almost none on a majority of the other customers. Though loyal customers need to be rewarded, the rest should not be ignored. It is the first-time fliers who need to be cultivated to become die-hard fans.

So how can airlines make every customer feel that he or she is center of the universe? Many make the mistake of assuming that delivering such an experience would require superfluous expenditure. In reality, consistency across multiple touch points is the key to winning a customer's heart. SilkAir, Singapore Airlines' regional subsidiary offers flights to holiday destinations in Southeast Asia. The airline's tagline is "where the world unwinds" and the aircraft cabin helps the customers settle into a holiday mood as soon as they enter the plane. Not only is the look and feel in line with the eXpectations, the stewardesses know almost everything a holiday-maker would want to learn about a destination, from the best restaurants to side trips—an eXperience, true to its word.

Brand eXpression: Engaging the Customer

Brand *eXpression* is often the overlooked aspect of branding which allows airlines to extend the engagement with their customers. It is the key to building familiarity with the brand through constant interaction to nurture loyal customers over time. The customers here belong to two main categories: external, which include passengers, analysts, governments, and even activists; and internal, which include pilots, staff, and crew.

For the external customer, the airline should formulate a strategy that ensures constant interaction with the customer, not just before he flies, but even after he has landed. Southwest has done this extremely well, by following some of their vocal customers on Twitter and engaging with them time to time. Such interactions encourage frank feedback and the openness leads to insights executives would not have had otherwise. Sometimes, airlines wonder if tapping on the latest technologies amounts to losing control over their brands. It is actually the exact opposite. As the brand consultant Mary Neumeier puts it, "It's not what *you* say it is. It's what *they* say it is".

Another aspect of brand *eXpression* relevant to the external customer is the ability to share the story. Companies often assume that word-of-mouth marketing or buzz is created automatically, but it is seldom the case. Customers must be empowered to share with the world stories of their experience with the airline, not just to sell the brand, but also to appear distinct in their own community. For example, kulula keeps additional safety cards at hand in case passengers nick some. The stolen cards are of course shared with friends and family. Nothing works better than an unbiased, customer recommendation to attract new business.

For the internal customer, brand *eXpression* helps develop an affinity with the staff that goes beyond rational facts and logical truths. In times of crises, it is the emotional attachment among the employees that keeps the company together. Hence, there should be constant efforts to build emotional bonds between the colleagues, either through regular non-work related activities, garnering and incorporating feedback, and simply making the airline a fun environment to work in. Emotional truths are intangible elements of an organization that inspire imagination, drive employee engagement, reduce churn and compel people to go beyond the call of duty. AirAsia and Southwest have done a terrific job at this by creating a family-like environment for their employees, and many of them have served these airlines for their entire careers.

Brand eXternalities: Dealing with Industry Uncertainty

Airlines have to deal with many issues beyond their control, much more than companies in other industries; from pilot unions and government regulations to events like 9/11. Even the sudden appearance of new competition on a premium route, or a competitor going bust often has little to do with an airline's own actions. Something as regular as flight delays due to weather are beyond the airlines' control as well. The fact is that every airline faces the same hurdles; it's how each one reacts that sets it apart from the competition.

Knee-jerk reactions are all too common in the airline industry. When the oil prices hit $140 per gallon in mid-2008, most U.S.-based airlines started charging for checked bags to drive ancillary revenues. They kept these charges for the long term due to the additional revenue brought in, despite oil prices hitting record lows recently. Interestingly, there was hardly a flutter from Southwest. The original low-cost carrier in the United States ironically is the only one not charging a checked-bag fee today. This is because dealing well with uncertainty requires a clear vision of what the brand stands for and what the airline can and cannot do.

A much-overlooked fact is that brand *eXternalities* are hidden opportunities to impress the customer beyond expectations, often by showing the human side of the company. When an AirAsia plane crashed in December 2014, Tony Fernandes led from the front, interacting and engaging with the public, media, and employees in a very personal manner. Resilience and flexibility are the keys to surviving industry-wide shocks and the better airlines are prepared to leverage on these to build their brand further.

By avoiding knee-jerk reactions to *eXternalities*, airlines also project trustworthiness. Reaction to sudden appearance of new competition or rises in fuel prices shouldn't change the customer experience drastically. Brand trust takes a long time to build and should not be breached overnight.

Brand eXecution: Consistency in Delivery

It is an art to deliver a great experience once, but delivering a consistently great experience over time is a science. This is because it requires meticulous planning and persistence to stay true to that plan in the face of external and internal pressures to change course. Brand *eXecution* requires an airline to stay true to its core brand personality in good times or bad and deliver a consistent experience. More than anything else, it is this consistency that builds trust among customers.

Good brand *eXecution* also requires consistency to be achieved across different product offerings and customer touch-points. The experience on a regional flight in an Embraer jet and a transatlantic flight in a Boeing 777 should not differ greatly. Similarly, if the airline staff is supposed to be chatty, they should be that way on the phone, at the check-in desk, and in flight. An airline should train its partners to interact with its customers in the same way as its staff.

Another aspect of good brand *eXecution* is the commitment to the brand ethos. The airline shouldn't be changing what the brand stands for too dramatically very often. A slow evolution is fine, as long as it resonates with the customers well.

Brand X-factor: Above and Beyond

Creating a brand *X-factor* is something that puts an airline in a league of its own and creates a halo around the brand. These are often the nuances that ensure that the airline stands apart from the competition and often leads to a cult status among its customers. Examples from other industries would be Harley-Davidson motorcycles and Apple products. Those who buy them swear by them. In the airline world, AirAsia, Singapore Airlines, and Southwest are outstanding examples of brands that have created an X-factor.

The common denominator in all of these examples is the creation of a brand icon, such as Tony Fernandes at AirAsia, the Singapore Girl at SIA, and peanuts at Southwest, which was the first airline to offer the industry's staple snack. Such icons often defy logic and create a magical attraction toward the brand. Better still, these icons can be leveraged to project the brand in ways generally difficult to articulate through traditional means. An ever-smiling Tony Fernandes can be seen at all AirAsia events, SIA's advertisements show more elegantly uniformed Singapore Girls than actual planes, and Southwest even has a blog named "Nuts about Southwest."

Something else that airlines do to create a warm feeling among their customers is to emphasize their net social impact by proactively managing their social and ethical stance. Great examples of this include AirAsia's free service to carry relief aid to Myanmar immediately after the cyclone Nargis ravaged the country or the work being done by AirAsia Foundation. Finnair's Helena Kaartinen put smiles on the faces of slum-dwelling children Mumbai by teaching them a dance and taking them on a flight to Delhi. Both of these initiatives reflect the dexterity and ingeniousness on the airlines' part to go beyond their everyday operations and make a positive impact on the society. It is efforts like these, which help gain the respect of current and future customers.

The X-factors add a personality to the brand. After all, personality inspires trust; and trust builds loyalty.

Conclusion

At the end of the day, deciding the most strategic branding approach for an airline is critical. Is increasing competition an issue? Is it perception, whereby the image of the airline is decreasing its ability to entice customers and a strong workforce? Whatever the situation, aligning with the suitable brand and business solution is essential.

The 6X model serves as a guide for this process, taking into account a number of factors unique to the airline industry, within and beyond the airlines' control. As portrayed by the airlines featured in *SOAR*, the aim shouldn't be to excel at each of the 6X factors, but rather choose a couple to focus on and then execute on them better than anyone else. That would help airlines become remarkable.

ACKNOWLEDGMENTS

A famous African saying goes, "it takes a village to raise a child." It also took a lot of flapping of wings by a lot of people in the last year to help *SOAR*, soar. I'm grateful to many people who believed in the idea of this book, the fact that its time had come, and to those who helped make it a reality.

As he boarded a flight to Beijing on the 12th of December 2011, Laird Robin Speculand, my longtime mentor seeded the idea of writing a book in me. He felt it was important to share the insights about airline marketing we were uncovering at SimpliFlying, with the rest of the world. He recommended I start writing a column with a leading publication and then publish a book subsequently. The monthly column came first – with Flight's Airline Business magazine – but the book took some time as the work and team at SimpliFlying continued to grow. But Robin kept asking me time and again, "when is the book coming out?", "when am I going to read it?" It was only a matter of time before I finally did it.

My deepest thanks to my writing partner and editor, Matthew Sharpe (Matt). While Matt has never written about aviation previously, he was open to hearing all the stories I had collected from the interviews with the various airlines, digest them and create chapter maps based on the themes highlighted. In the couple of months leading to the publication *SOAR*, he made this project a top priority, dedicating almost all his time to it. Matt is a true professional and it has been a pleasure working with him on the book. Ultimately, the chapters were ready for print in record time, and by the end of it, Matt probably became a bit of an #avgeek too.

I also had the pleasure of working with an A-list publishing team at IdeaPress Publishing. I had known Rohit Bhargava, its founder, since the early days of SimpliFlying. When I decided to write a book on airline marketing, he was one of the first publishers I bounced off the ideas with and he was on board from the get go. Rohit himself is a bestselling author and a renowned marketing expert. He shared lessons learnt from his previous projects throughout the time I worked on *SOAR* and those were invaluable. His team of layout designers, proofreaders and all-things-publishing took care of aspects that I was not familiar with at the start of the project. Special thanks also to Marnie McMahon for coordinating all the different moving pieces of the publishing process with finesse.

Shubhodeep Pal, an integral part of the SimpliFlying team for over five years was an integral part of this book too. I'm eternally grateful to him for reading through every single chapter and even helping write one. He and I share a special bond, and I'm glad he never minced words when trying to get a point across. His critical gaze across the words helped improve the quality of the content in *SOAR* tremendously.

The rest of the SimpliFlying team deserves credit too. All of them helped me transcribe parts of the interviews – Dirk did it all manually in a single sitting! He was also instrumental in taking care of all the local logistics for the book launch in London. Guen and

Baiba pulled together an exhaustive list of journalists and bloggers who had ever written about us, and those based in the UK. Marco and Ravi helped look through the chapters too, while delivering MasterClasses and preparing reports. Most importantly, in the months leading up to the book being published, it was thanks to the SimpliFlying team looking after almost every project that I was able to completely dedicate myself to *SOAR*.

The insights in the book are based on almost a hundred interviews with airline executives done around the world over a year. I'm thankful to the executive staff and Communication departments of the airlines in the book for coordinating my complicated itineraries and all the interviews with the senior executives. Thanks to Sandra Freeman at Air New Zealand in helping coordinate flights and appointments. I even got lucky with a seat next to the New Zealand Prime Minister on my way to Auckland. Melanie Jones and Richard West at Southwest went above and beyond to ensure I spoke with the right people. Richard, by the way, is a treasure trove of information about Southwest and remembers dates off his head! Laajarinne Tuuli, Juha Jarvinen for making the interviews happen at Finnair and Helena Kaartinen, whose stories brought tears to my eyes. Emre and Neset bey at Turkish Airlines for working through the Christmas and New Year holidays on the book. Shaun Pozyn at kulula for ensuring the right people share their stories, and following up with a ton of resources. Audrey Petriny and Rudy Khaw at AirAsia for ensuring I got a slot onto Tony Fernandes' diary. Barbara Fisa and Tania Villa at Vueling were very helpful in securing interviews at a short notice. And finally Nicholas Ionides at Singapore Airlines, who not only coordinated all the interviews but also even drove me to the airline headquarters in his car so that I could skip the long security lines. Each of these people and their teams ensured quick turnarounds for the chapters once they were written so that the dates for publishing did not slip.

I'm humbled by the words of industry stalwarts who agreed to read excerpts of the book ahead of time and provide endorsements for *SOAR*. David Meerman Scott, Chris Brogan, Dr. Bernd Schmitt and Allen Adamson are all I've looked up to as marketing and branding experts. Dr. Mario Hardy continues to travel and spot more exotic coffee shops than anyone else I know. Gianfranco "Panda" Beting who is a complete aviation geek like I am. Jeff Cacy, Patrick Baudis and Mark Lapidus – all of whom I've had the pleasure of working with in the past few years. Nicola Lange and Mary Ellen Jones - just a couple of the ladies exemplifying the lean-in movement within aviation. Michael Blunt from Oneworld, who was very kind with his words. Angela Gittens who has been an ardent supporter of our work at SimpliFlying for many years. And Patrick Murphy, who probably knows more about the industry than I can ever hope to learn.

Finally, this book wouldn't have become a reality without the constant support of my wife, Prajakta. While the book was in the process of being written, we participated in two family weddings back in India, visited parents across the continent, moved from Ottawa to Toronto and set up our new place. Prajakta constantly checked in with me on the progress of the book and helped me clarify my often-cloudy vision for some chapters. She calmed me down when I grew increasingly frustrated due to the tedious nature of the publishing process. I'm thankful to her for being understanding about the calls I took with Matt while shopping for baby cribs in Ikea or the travels from Finland to New Zealand that took me away for weeks. Ultimately, this book is as much a testament to her willpower, as mine. And of course, Sanaa, who would walk in to the office, as I was busy editing, and bring the joy back into writing.

Our special thanks to all the people below for sharing unique insights and passionate stories while being interviewed for the book.

Southwest Airlines
1. Anne Murray, Senior Director, Marketing
2. Kristi Owens, Director, SWA University
3. Cheryl Hughey, Managing Director, Culture Services
4. Shari Conaway, Director, People
5. Lisa Goode, Senior Director, Communication & Outreach
6. Gary Kelly, Chairman, Chief Executive Officer, President
7. Connor Hughey, Senior Representative, Customer Relations & Rapid Rewards
8. Mike Hafner, Vice President, Customer Services
9. Helen Limpitlaw, Director, Marketing

Special thanks to Melanie Jones, Richard West, Carla Lemire from Communications.

AirAsia
1. Tony Fernandes, Co-founder and Group CEO
2. Yap Mun Ching, Head of AirAsia Foundation
3. Joyce Lai Group Head, Duty Free & Merchandise
4. Suhaila Hassan Group Head, Cabin Crew Department
5. Kugan A/L Tangiisuran, Co-Pilot
6. Capt. Chin Nyok San, Group Head of Cargo
7. Banyat Hansakul Head of Engineering, AirAsia Thailand

Air New Zealand

1. Mele Sulunga, Auckland Domestic Customer Service Agent
2. Scott Bishop, Head of Customer Innovation
3. Dave McRobie, Innovation Manager
4. Kerry Reeves, Head of Aircraft Programmes
5. Jodie Williams, Head of Global Brand
6. Mike Tod, Chief Marketing & Customer Officer
7. Christopher Luxon, CEO

Turkish Airlines

1. Arif Ali Cizmecioglu, Customer Experience Manager
2. Akif Konar, Chief Commercial Officer
3. Zeki Cukur, SVP Catering & Inflight Products
4. Neset Dereli, Interactive Marketing Communication Manager
5. Inanc Emre Albayrak, Interactive Marketing Communication Supervisor
6. Dr.Temel Kotil, CEO

Singapore Airlines

1. Foo Juat Fang, Assistant Manager Cabin Crew Training
2. Marvin Tan, Senior Vice President Product & Services
3. Michelle Ong, Flight Attendant
4. Nicholas Ionides, Divisional Vice President Public Affairs
5. Goh Choon Phong, CEO
6. Laird Robin Speculand, SIA PPS Club Solitaire member
7. Khoa Huynh, SIA PPS Club member

Kulula
1. Brian Kitchin, Executive Manager, Sales
2. Shaun Pozyn, Executive Manager, Marketing
3. Cherese Wansink, Head of Design
4. Tracey McCreadie, Service Delivery Manager
5. Erik Venter, CEO
6. Mike Ilsley, Executive Manager of IT, Contact Centre and CIO

Finnair
1. Pekka Vauramo, CEO
2. Juha Jarvinen, CCO
3. Jarkko Konttinen, VP Product Development & Ancillary Business
4. Heléne Lidström, VP Brand & Marketing
5. Taru Kettunen, Brand Manager
6. Helena Kaartinen, Senior Cabin Crew
7. Suvi Saarela, Cabin Crew
8. Sami Laine, Co-Pilot
9. Olli Lehtonen, Former Marketing Consultant
10. Vertti Kivi, CEO, dSign Vertti Kivi & Co

BIBLIOGRAPHY

In addition to the interviews we conducted with personnel at each airline, we consulted a variety of other sources in the course of researching this book. They are listed below.

SOUTHWEST

Baer, Jay. "Six Unforgettable Lessons from the Southwest Airlines Social Media Crisis." Medium. https://medium.com/convince-and-convert/6-unforgettable-lessons-from-the-southwest-airlines-social-media-crisis-e6b6d8870c8c#.876rl4d64 (accessed September 23, 2016).

Barnum, Winifred, Gumwrappers and Goggles: the Tale of a Jet. Summit Publishing Company, 1982.

Carey, Susan. "Southwest Airlines Launches 'Transfarency' Campaign." The *Wall Street Journal*. http://www.wsj.com/articles/southwest-airlines-launches-new-ad-campaign-1444323893 (accessed September 23, 2016).

Constine, Josh. "Facebook Climbs to 1.59 Billion Users and Crushes Q4 Estimates with $5.8B Revenue." https://techcrunch.com/2016/01/27/facebook-earnings-q4-2015/ (accessed September 23, 2016).

Dostis, Melanie. "Kevin Smith Ends Boycott with Southwest Airlines." New York Daily News. http://www.nydailynews.com/entertainment/gossip/

kevin-smith-ends-boycott-southwest-airlines-article-1.2644618 (accessed September 23, 2016).

Gambino, Lauren. "Southest Airlines Criticized After Incidents Involving Middle Eastern Passengers." The Guardian. https://www. theguardian.com/us-news/2015/nov/21/southwest-airlines-muslim-middle-eastern-passengers (accessed September 23, 2016).

Kamer, Foster. "Update: The Kevin Smith Southwest Airlines Fat-Flight Tweakout of Epic Proportions." Gawker. http://gawker. com/5471463/update-the-kevin-smith-southwest-airlines-fat-flight-tweakout-of-epic-proportion (accessed September 23, 2016).

Mutzabough, Ben. "Southwest Airlines Flight Woes Cascade into Friday." USA Today. http://www.usatoday.com/story/travel/flights/todayinthesky/2016/07/22/southwest-airlines-flight-woes-cascade-into-friday/87430038/ (accessed September 23, 2016).

Revesz, Rachel. "Muslim Woman Kicked Off Plane as Flight Attendant Said She 'Did Not Feel Comfortable' with the Passenger." Independent. http://www.independent.co.uk/news/world/americas/muslim-woman-kicked-off-plane-as-flight-attendant-said-she-did-not-feel-comfortable-with-the-a6986661.html (accessed September 22, 2016).

Robbins, Chris. "Southwest Airlines: a Culture of Hospitality." LinkedIn. https://www.linkedin.com/pulse/southwest-airlines-culture-hospitality-chris-robbins (accessed September 22, 2016).

Stack, Liam. "College Student Is Removed from Flight After Speaking Arabic on Plane." The New York Times. http://www.nytimes.com/2016/04/17/us/student-speaking-arabic-removed-southwest-airlines-plane.html?_r=0 (accessed September 22, 2016).

Wald, Matthew L. "M. Lamar Muse, 86, Dies; Led Southwest Airlines." The New York Times. http://www.nytimes.com/2007/02/07/business/07muse.html?_r=0 (accessed August 12, 2016).

Weber, Julie. "How Southwest Airlines Hires Such Dedicated People." Harvard Business Review. https://hbr.org/2015/12/

how-southwest-airlines-hires-such-dedicated-people (accessed
August 13, 2016).

"About Southwest." Southwest Airlines. https://www.southwest.com/
html/about-southwest/index.html?int= (accessed September 22,
2016).

"Bottom of the Class: America's Airlines Are Introducing a Class
Below Economy." The Economist. http://www.economist.com/blogs/
gulliver/2016/02/bottom-class (accessed August 13, 2016).

"Colleen Barrett." Wikipedia. https://en.wikipedia.org/wiki/Colleen_
Barrett (accessed August 12, 2016).

"'Flying While Muslim': Profiling Fears After Arabic Speaker Removed
from Plane." NPR. http://www.npr.org/2016/04/20/475015239/
flying-while-muslim-profiling-fears-after-arabic-speaker-removed-
from-plane (accessed September 22, 2016).

"Global Air Traffic and Top Airlines (IATA)." IMM International.
http://www.imm-international.com/global-air-traffic-top-airlines-
2016-iata/ (accessed September 22, 2016).

"New Logo, Identity, and Livery for Southwest Airlines." Brand New.
http://www.underconsideration.com/brandnew/archives/new_
logo_identity_and_livery_for_southwest_airlines_by_lippincott.
php#.V-QW8rWZDxQ (accessed September 22, 2016).

Southwest Airlines. http://www.transfarency.com/ (accessed September 23, 2016).

"Southwest Airlines Accused of Profiling Muslims." The Economist.
http://www.economist.com/blogs/gulliver/2015/11/nothing-fear-ex-
cept-fear-itself (accessed September 23, 2016).

"Southwest Airlines' Colleen Barrett Flies High on Fuel Hedging and
'Servant Leadership.'" Knowledge@Wharton. http://knowledge.
wharton.upenn.edu/article/southwest-airlines-colleen-barrett-flies-
high-on-fuel-hedging-and-servant-leadership/ (accessed September
22, 2016).

"Southwest Airlines Offers New Boarding Option." Southwest Airlines. http://swamedia.com/releases/southwest-airlines-offers-new-boarding-option (accessed September 22, 2016).

"Southwest Airlines Recognized as One of the Best Places to Work in 2015." Southwest Airlines. http://swamedia.com/releases/southwest-airlines-recognized-as-one-of-best-places-to-work-in?l=en-US (accessed September 22, 2016).

"Southwest Airlines: Transfarency." https://www.youtube.com/watch?v=QncggSfezL0 (accessed September 23, 2016).

"Southwest Airlines Unveils Its New Look, Same Heart." Southwest Airlines. http://heart.swamedia.com/news/index.html (accessed September 22, 2016).

"Southwest Alters Boarding Process." *The New York Times*. http://www.nytimes.com/2007/09/20/business/20air.html?_r=0 (accessed September 22, 2016).

"The Southwest Boarding Process." YouTube. https://www.youtube.com/watch?v=X2B7EilM0pk (accessed September 22, 2016).

"Southwest's New Ad Mocks Other Airlines' Fees." Fortune. http://fortune.com/2015/10/08/southwest-ad-fees/?iid=leftrail (accessed September 23, 2016).

Knatchwell, Phyllis. "transfarency." Urban Dictionary. http://www.urbandictionary.com/define.php?term=transfarency (accessed September 23, 2016).

"Welcome to the Southwest Airlines Community!" Southwest Airlines. https://community.southwest.com/ (accessed September 22, 2016).

FINNAIR

Laufik, Michele. "What We Love About Finnair's New Aircraft." ShermansTravel. https://blog.shermanstravel.com/2016/what-we-love-about-finnairs-new-aircraft-northern-lights-projection-included/ (accessed June 20, 2016).

"Finnair's Mr. Europe Wins Prize in Japan." Finnair. http://www.
finnairgroup.com/mediaen/mediaen_7.html?Id=rss_527363.html
(accessed June 19, 2016).

"Flight of Fantasy Bollywood Dance." YouTube. https://www.youtube.
com/watch?v=KBe3MYExDVU (accessed June 18, 2016).

"Marimekko Makeover for Finnish Airline." Dezeen. http://www.
dezeen.com/2012/10/29/marimekko-makeover-for-finnish-air-
line-finnair/ (accessed January 15, 2016).

"Match Made in HEL 2014." YouTube. https://www.youtube.com/
watch?v=H9sjYnSQFaE (accessed June 18, 2016).

"Space Alive." Aircraft Interiors International Annual Showcase 2016.

"Story Behind the Flight of Fantasy." YouTube. https://www.youtube.
com/watch?v=f5vS1zC3e0k (accessed June 18, 2016).

"Surprise Dance on Finnair Flight to Celebrate India's Republic Day."
YouTube. https://www.youtube.com/watch?v=mEsnb3kUDAw
(accessed June 18, 2016).

"Thule." Wikipedia. https://en.wikipedia.org/wiki/Thule (accessed
June 20, 2016).

AIRASIA

Datta, Kanika. "Tea with BS: Tony Fernandes." Business Standard.
http://www.business-standard.com/article/opinion/tea-with-bs-to-
ny-fernandes-110051800033_1.html (accessed July 17, 2016).

Mertens, Brian. "Flying on a Budget." Forbes. http://www.forbes.com/
global/2010/1220/features-airasia-tony-fernandes-flying-on-budget.
html (accessed July 15, 2016).

Clampet, Jason. "AirAsia's CEO Is Becoming the Model for Airline
Leaders During a Crisis." Skift. https://skift.com/2015/01/02/aira-
sias-ceo-is-becoming-the-model-for-airline-leaders-during-a-crisis/
(accessed March 23, 2016).

Singh, Kulwant; Pangarkar, Nitin; and Heracleous, Loizos. Business
Strategy In Asia: A Casebook. Lulu Press, 2014.

Nigam, Shashank. "Want your new route to make headlines? Bring
Richard Branson on-board, like AirAsia X did in Perth!" http://
simpliflying.com/2013/want-your-new-route-to-make-headlines-
bring-richard-branson-on-board-like-airasia-x-did-in-perth/
(accessed July 16, 2016)

"AirAsia." Wikipedia. https://en.wikipedia.org/wiki/AirAsia (accessed
July 16, 2016).

AirAsia Foundation. http://www.airasiafoundation.com/ (accessed
July 18, 2016).

"Richard Branson Does Drag After Losing Bet." CNN. http://www.
cnn.com/2013/05/13/travel/branson-flight-attendant/ (accessed July
18, 2016).

TURKISH AIRLINES

"Interview: Dr. Temel Kotil, CEO, Turkish Airlines." Air Transport
News. http://atn.aero/analysis.pl?id=1739 (accessed August 7, 2016).

Snyder, Brett. "Turkish Airlines Has to Be Concerned About Its
Future." Cranky Flier. http://crankyflier.com/2016/07/18/turkish-
airlines-has-to-be-concerned-about-its-future/ (accessed August 7,
2016).

"15 Reasons Istanbul and San Francisco Are Long-Lost Sister Cities."
BuzzFeed. https://www.buzzfeed.com/turkishairlines/istan-
bul-and-san-francisco?utm_term=.janGjNezk8#.wpLeP7Z5Nd
(accessed August 9, 2016).

Nigam, Shashank. "Turkish Airlines "Widen Your World" blog shares
crewsourced destination tips with travellers." http://simpliflying.
com/2014/turkish-airlines-widen-world-blog-shares-crew-
sourced-destination-tips-travelers/ (accessed August 8, 2016).

Mehra, Vishal. "Turkish Airlines launches Istanbul to San Francisco
route with creative marketing." http://simpliflying.com/2015/

turkish-airlines-istanbul-san-francisco-route-marketing/ (accessed August 7, 2016).

Pal, Shubhodeep. "Turkish Airlines Invest on Board Adds a Twist to Online Crowdsourcing and Connects Entrepreneurs with High-Value Investors." http://simpliflying.com/2013/turkish-airlines-invest-on-board/ (accessed August 9, 2016)

Nigam, Shashank. "Kobe vs Messi selfie shootout advertisement by Turkish Airlines goes viral (and 6 ideas to improve it)." http://simpliflying.com/2013/kobe-messi-selfie-shootout-advertisement-turkish-airlines/ (accessed August 10, 2016).

Nigam, Shashank. " Turkish Airlines International CIP Lounge in Istanbul – possibly the best Star Alliance lounge there is!" http://simpliflying.com/2012/pics-turkish-airlines-international-cip-lounge-in-istanbul-possibly-the-best-star-alliance-lounge-there-is/ (accessed August 11, 2016)

Nigam, Shashank. "Creating the best food in Economy Class: Turkish Airlines Do&Co take us behind the scenes." http://simpliflying.com/2010/creating-the-best-food-in-economy-class-turkish-airlines-doco-take-us-behind-the-scenes/ (accessed August 11, 2016)

Nigam, Shashank. "Turkish Airlines Business Class." https://simplisoar.exposure.co/turkish-airlines-business-class/ (accessed August 10, 2016).

Nigam, Shashank. "Lounge Istanbul by Turkish Airlines." https://simplisoar.exposure.co/lounge-istanbul-by-turkish-airlines (accessed August 11, 2016).

"Kobe vs. Messi: Legends on Board." YouTube. https://www.youtube.com/watch?v=ruav0KvQOOg (accessed August 10, 2016).

"Kobe vs. Messi: the Selfie Shootout." YouTube. https://www.youtube.com/watch?v=jhFqSlvbKAM (accessed August 10, 2016).

"Turkish Airlines Presents Startup Class." YouTube. https://www.youtube.com/watch?v=8kDlkbq0FYM (accessed August 8, 2016).

KULULA

Brown, Genevieve Shaw. "Your Fourth Wife Flies Free on Kulula Airlines." ABC News. http://abcnews.go.com/blogs/lifestyle/2012/04/your-fourth-wife-flies-free-on-kulula-airlines/ (accessed July 27, 2016).

Nigam, Shashank. "South Africa's Kulula Airlines goes back to basics with Flying 101 re-branding." http://simpliflying.com/2010/south-africas-kulula-airlines-goes-back-to-basics-with-flying-101-re-branding/ (accessed July 28, 2016).

"Comair (South Africa)." Wikipedia. https://en.wikipedia.org/wiki/Comair_(South_Africa) (accessed August 1, 2016).

"Flying 101." Snopes.com. http://www.snopes.com/photos/airplane/kulula.asp (accessed July 27, 2016).

"It's Official: Sepp Blatter Flies Kulula!" kulula.com. http://www.kulula.com/press-room/18-june-2010-its-oficial-sepp-blatter-flies-kulula (accessed July 28, 2016).

"Kulula 101." kulula.com. http://www.kulula.com/brand/kulula101 (accessed July 28, 2016).

Nigam, Shashank. "Kulula.com lures South Africans with authentic advertising." http://simpliflying.com/2008/kulula-com-lures-south-african-travelers-with-authentic-advertising/ (accessed July 28, 2016).

Nigam, Shashank. "Kulula, the most fun airline brand in the world?" http://simpliflying.com/2010/kulula-airlines-the-most-fun-airline-brand-in-the-world/ (accessed July 28, 2016).

"Kulula's Humorous Safety Demonstration." YouTube. https://www.youtube.com/watch?v=XhWmN4bHOK8 (accessed July 26, 2016).

"Luggage Troubles." YouTube. https://www.youtube.com/watch?v=zdXBrcqjru4 (accessed July 28, 2016).

"Skip the Queue and Check-in Online from Anywhere." kulula.com. http://www.kulula.com/brand/kulula101 (accessed July 26, 2016).

SINGAPORE AIRLINES

Nigam, Shashank. "Six Steps to Building a Swashbuckling Airline Brand." SimpliFlying. http://simpliflying.com/airline-branding-whitepaper/ (accessed June 8, 2016).

Ramchandani, Nisha. "Keeping It a Great Way to Fly." The Business Times. http://www.businesstimes.com.sg/the-raffles-conversation/keeping-it-a-great-way-to-fly (accessed January 31, 2106).

Waldron, Greg. "Connecting the Globe." Airline Business. July–August 2015.

"At Singapore Airlines, No Detail Is Too Small." YouTube. https://www.youtube.com/watch?v=wt99b5ccwqk (accessed June 13, 2016).

"Singapore Airlines." Wikipedia. https://en.wikipedia.org/wiki/Singapore_Airlines (accessed June 12, 2016).

"Singapore Airlines Flight 006." Wikipedia. https://en.wikipedia.org/wiki/Singapore_Airlines_Flight_006 (accessed June 15, 2016).

Heracleous, Loizos, Wirtz, Jochen. "The Globe: Singapore Airlines' balancing act." https://hbr.org/2010/07/the-globe-singapore-airlines-balancing-act (accessed June 14, 2016).

VUELING

Garcia, Marisa. "6 Insights From Vueling's CEO on Running the Contrarian Low-Cost Carrier." Skift. https://skift.com/2015/09/24/6-insights-from-vuelings-ceo-on-running-the-contrarian-low-cost-carrier/ (accessed September 19, 2016).

Mackenzie, Scott. "Review: Vueling Airlines from Barcelona to Granada." Travel Codex. http://www.travelcodex.com/2015/10/review-vueling-airlines-from-barcelona-to-granada/ (accessed September 27, 2016).

Serusi, Marco. "Lessons Learned in Social Media: How Vueling Should Have Dealt with the Hijack That Never Was." Tnooz. https://www. tnooz.com/article/lessons-learned-in-social-media-how-vueling-should-have-dealt-with-the-hijack-that-never-was/ (accessed September 16, 2016).

Serusi, Marco. "Vueling's Business Class Drives Awareness Creatively." Simpliflying. http://simpliflying.com/2012/vueling-business-class-drives-awareness-creatively-the-cloud-that-fell-from-the-sky/

"The Last Word in Cost Control." Airlines International. http://airlines.iata.org/ceo-interviews/the-last-word-in-cost-control (accessed September 18, 2016).

"IAG Has Its Best-Ever Profit in 2015 Helped by Fuel and Strategic Vision and Pragmatism." Centre for Aviation. http://centreforaviation.com/analysis/iag-has-its-best-ever-profit-in-2015-helped-by-fuel-and-strategic-vision-and-pragmatism-269039 (accessed September 23, 2016).

"'Miscommunication' Sparks Plane Hijack Alert, Dutch F-16 Scrambled." RT News. https://www.rt.com/news/dutch-plane-hostages-schiphol-849/ (accessed September 18, 2016).

"Qatar Airways and Vueling to Code Share as LCC Partnerships Establish New Models." Centre for Aviation. http://centreforaviation.com/analysis/qatar-airways-and-vueling-to-codeshare-as-lcc-partnerships-establish-new-models-300689 (accessed September 23, 2016).

"Vueling Is World's First Airline with a Geo-Localisation Technology App for Apple Watch." Vueling News. http://vuelingnews.com/vueling-is-worlds-first-airline-with-a-geo-localisation-technology-app-for-apple-watch/?lang=en (accessed September 18, 2016).

"Vueling's New CEO Only Needs to Stay Ahead of Rival LCCs on Service Quality and Keep Cutting Costs." Centre for Aviation. http://centreforaviation.com/analysis/vuelings-new-ceo-only-needs-to-stay-ahead-of-rival-lccs-on-service-quality-and-keep-cutting-costs-254676 (accessed September 23, 2016).

"Your Custom Travel with Vueling Fares." Vueling. http://www.vueling. com/en/vueling-services/vueling-fares (accessed September 27, 2016).

AIR NEW ZEALAND

Rajagopal, Arun. "Brand Leadership Lessons from Air New Zealand." Arun Rajagopal. https://arunrajagopal.com/2010/01/26/air-new-zealand/ (accessed August 6, 2016).

Wassener, Bettina. "Airline Has Nothing to Hide. Really." *The New York Times.* http://www.nytimes.com/2009/06/30/business/30air. html?_r=0 (accessed August 7, 2016).

Air New Zealand: Celebrating 75 Years. Auckland: Bauer Media Group, 2014.

"Air New Zealand Fairy to be Showcased Among the Best at Air New Zealand Conference." Air New Zealand. http://www.airnewzealand. com.au/press-release-2013-air-new-zealand-fairy-to-be-showcased-among-the-best-at-google-conference (accessed August 8, 2016).

"Air New Zealand: Happy Hour." YouTube. https://www.youtube.com/ watch?v=BZLBY3lYtsQ (accessed August 5, 2016).

"Air New Zealand's AirBand™a World First." Air New Zealand. http:// www.airnewzealand.co.nz/press-release-2015-airnz-airband-a-world-first (accessed August 6, 2016).

"Ansett Australia." Wikipedia. https://en.wikipedia.org/wiki/Ansett_ Australia (accessed August 5, 2016).

"Bare Essentials of Safety from Air New Zealand." YouTube. https:// www.youtube.com/watch?v=fwBfOSZKipk (accessed August 5, 2016).

"David Hasselhoff: On the Skycouch with Rico." YouTube. https:// www.youtube.com/watch?v=pLq1XR88EtQ (accessed August 5, 2016).

"First Peoples in Māori Tradition: Kupe." Te Ara: The Encyclopedia of New Zealand. http://www.teara.govt.nz/en/first-peoples-in-mao-ri-tradition/page-6 (accessed August 4, 2016).

"Fit to Fly with Richard Simmons." YouTube. https://www.youtube.com/watch?v=IgJg4-Ea_wI (accessed August 5, 2016).

"Lindsay Lohan: On the Skycouch with Rico." YouTube. https://www.youtube.com/watch?v=pds0fOiKs1U (accessed August 5, 2016).

"The Most Epic Safety Video Ever Made." YouTube. https://www.youtube.com/watch?v=qOw44VFNk8Y (accessed August 5, 2016).

"Nothing to Hide." YouTube. https://www.youtube.com/watch?v=KS06IW1bdLg (accessed August 5, 2016).

"Rico's Murderer Busted!" YouTube. https://www.youtube.com/watch?v=7NJlLA7eGBI (accessed August 5, 2016).

"Unfiltered: Christopher Luxon, CEO Air New Zealand." Vimeo. https://vimeo.com/unfilterednz/review/169742439/0f8ac26134 (accessed August 10, 2016).

ABOUT THE AUTHOR

Widely hailed as a pioneer in airline branding, Shashank Nigam is the Founder and CEO of SimpliFlying. His team woven together across time zones with an enviable culture belies SimpliFlying's status as one of the most sought-after marketing strategy firm in the industry today. In mere six years, they have helped over 75 airlines and airports become remarkable.

Nigam is the youngest winner of the Global Brand Leadership Award and regularly addresses senior aviation executives across the globe. His impassioned, lateral and honest perspectives on airline marketing have become food for thought through interviews in over 100 media outlets, including the BBC, CNBC, Reuters and Bloomberg, and leading publications like the Wall Street Journal and New York Times. His nuanced insights feature in his monthly column in Flight's Airline Business.

An alumnus of Singapore Management University and Carnegie Mellon University in Information Systems Management and Business Management, he is a true globe-trotter. He was born in India, grew up in Singapore, lived in inspiring locations including Boston and Kampala and is currently based in Toronto with his wife and daughter. Soon to be a second-time dad, he still manages to keep his first loves alive – seeking out good design, inventing recipes in the kitchen and watching and playing cricket.

INDEX

A

AirAsia, 3, 6, 53–69, 193, 199
  brand awareness and, 107
  Branson, Richard and, 97
  cabin crew of, 63–64
  comparison with Kulula.com,
    107–108
  cost-saving initiatives of, 56
  empowering of employees at, 60–64
  flat structure at, 59
  hiring practices of, 67
  ordinary people and, 65–68
  provision of services to ASEAN
    countries, 57–58
  rise of, 53–57
  safety of, 56
  6X analysis of, 69
  strengths of, 55–56
  25-minute turnaround of, 56–57
  2014 crash and, 64–65, 96
AirAsia Flight QZ 8501, crash of, 64–65,
    96
AirAsia Foundation, 58, 66, 67
Airband, 183
Air Canada, 141
AirFrance, 125–126
Air India, 143
Airline industry, 4
Air New Zealand, 6, 117, 142, 169–186,
    188, 200
  Airband and, 183
  "Bare Essentials" video for, 174, 175,
    186
  CEOs of, 170
  customer experience at, 171–173
  employee empowerment at, 177–182
  High Performance Engagement

Project at, 180–181
  in-flight chat system on, 106
  Kupe Project at, 169, 171, 179–180
  "Nothing to Hide" advertising by, 104
  Premium Economy Spaceseat at, 176
  rebirth of, 169–171
  Rico (mascot) on, 106, 175, 176, 177
  safety at, 173–177
  6X analysis of, 185–186
  Skycouch on, 105, 106, 172–173, 174,
    176, 186
  technology and, 182–185
Air Southwest Co., 10
AirTran Airways, Southwest acquisition
  of, 17, 19
American Airlines, 1, 2, 23
America Online, 54
Anderson, Lisa, 23, 24, 26
Ansett, 169–170
Apple, 13–14, 193
  Watch, 157
Arto Saari Invitational skateboard event,
  47
Asian hospitality, 130
Asian market, position of Finnair in,
  44–46
Association of Southeast Asian Nations
  (ASEAN) countries, AirAsia services
  to, 57–58
Atmosphere Research Group, 2

B

Balmain, Pierre, 129
Braniff, legal action against Southwest, 9
Barnum, Winfred, 9
Barrett, Colleen, 12, 19, 23, 25, 33, 34
Basukettoke, 78

6X analysis of, 51–52
social network presence and, 46
FLY (Freedom, LUV, You), 19
"Flying 101" plane, 100, 111–113, 123
Four Seasons, 184
Frontier, passenger dissatisfaction with, 27
Fyfe, Rob, 170, 174, 178

G
Galán, Miguel Angel, 165
Gawde, Manish, 48
Generic marketing principles, 4
Goh, Choon Phong, 128, 133–134, 138, 139, 142
Google, 156
testing of Vueling's mobile booking apps by, 157
Google Glass, 139
Grangzhou, 46
Grylls, Bear, 175
GSD&M (ad agency), 28
Gulliver, The Economist's travel blog, 27
Gumwrappers and Goggles, 9–11

H
Haasselhoff, David, 106, 177
Hafner, Mike, 12–13, 16–17, 23, 25–26, 33
Harley-Davidson motorcycles, 193
Harteveldt, Henry, 2
Hassan, Suhaila, 63–64
Hastings, Reed, 184
Heathrow Airport, 54
Helsinki
Arto Saari Invitational skateboard event at, 47
Finnair lounge in, 43
position as a hub, 45
Helsinki-Vantaa Airport, 37, 39, 49
Hughey, Cheryl, 17
Hughey, Connor, 17
Huynh, Khoa, 131

I
Iaconi-Stewart, Luca, 103, 143
IDEO, 172
Ilsley, Mike, 110
IndiGo, Southwest model and, 30
Instagram, 31, 84
Internet journalism, 60
Istanbul, 74
Istanbul Ataturk, 88

J
Jackson, Peter, 175
Jarvinen, Juha, 43, 49
Jet Blue, 2
JetStar, Southwest model and, 30
Johor Bahru, 58

K
Kaartinen, Helena, 37–38, 39, 45, 46, 48–49, 193
Kardashian, Kim, 177
Kelleher, Herb, 9, 10, 11–12, 15, 19, 34, 91
Kelly, Gary, 14, 16, 19, 23, 29
Kennedy, John F., 155
Kivi, Vertti, 42, 49
King, Rollin, 9, 11
Kitchin, Brian, 108, 109, 123
KLM Royal Dutch Airlines, 44
carbon emissions of, 45
"Kobe v. Messi: the Selfie Shootout," 79–80, 98
Konar, Akif, 76
Konttinen, Jarkko, 38–39, 41–42, 44, 46
Kotil, Temel, 77, 86–87, 90
Kuala Lumpur International Airport, 3, 57
Kulula.com, 6, 107–123, 201
advertising by, 101
brand identity of, 119, 121
business class on, 121
comparison with AirAsia, 107–108
culture wall in crew briefing room of, 101
Discovery Health and, 121